PIES, BAKES AND CASSEROLES

A delicious collection of tasty vegetable dishes, together with original and appetizing ideas for toppings with which to ring the changes.

Recipes illustrated on cover:
1. Brussel Sprout and Almond Casserole (page 35)
2. Bean and Vegetable Cobbler (page 71)
3. Stuffed Cabbage Leaves (page 96)
4. Winter Vegetable Casserole (page 68)
5. Broad Bean and Carrot Pie (page 109)

PIES, BAKES AND CASSEROLES

by

PAMELA DIXON

Illustrated by Clive Birch

THORSONS PUBLISHERS LIMITED
Wellingborough, Northamptonshire

First published 1983

British Library Cataloguing in Publication Data

Dixon, Pamela
  Pies, bakes and casseroles.
  1. Vegetarian cookery
  I. Title
  641.5'636   TX837

ISBN 0-7225-0763-1

Printed in Great Britain by
Richard Clay (The Chaucer Press) Ltd,
Bungay, Suffolk

CONTENTS

Wholefoods, quite simply, are foods in their natural state — nothing added, nothing taken away. In this age of mass-production foods, wholefoods are not always easy to obtain. But as nutritionalists and doctors become increasingly convinced of their value in building and maintaining health, so their availability is fast improving.

Include as many natural, unadulterated foods as you can in your day to day eating pattern, and discover not just exciting new tastes and a fresh approach to mealtimes, but better health too.

INTRODUCTION

Vegetarian food has a double appeal these days. Those for whom it is already part of a way of life need no further convincing, but thousands of others are beginning to enjoy meals without meat because of the simple realization that they make the best use of the world's food resources. Newcomers to meatless meals are often surprised at the wide variety of ingredients available, from eggs, cheese and other dairy produce, to grains, nuts and pulses and the full delicious range of vegetables, fruits and herbs.

We are fortunate nowadays in being able to buy vegetables from all over the world, including the more exotic items, such as aubergines (eggplants) and peppers, which have found their way in to the local greengrocer only in the last twenty years or so. Because everyone travels, and because more immigrants from eastern countries have made their homes in the west, it is now possible to buy a wider variety of dried peas and beans and a vast range of herbs and spices, too.

Any keen cook who has a garden, or even a few tubs or window boxes, can cultivate fresh herbs for use through the summer. They make a great difference to the flavour of a dish. You can never have too much parsley — grow a clump wherever there is a patch of rich, moist soil to spare. Try, too, sage and thyme which are undemanding, fennel, rosemary and annual marjoram. Sweet basil, one of the loveliest and most aromatic herbs, needs plenty of warmth and often does best in pots on a sunny window sill.

I don't propose to enter into the butter versus margarine controversy. In some recipes the flavour of butter makes a real contribution to success, whereas in others it is less important. My own compromise is to use vegetable oil and polyunsaturated margarine wherever possible. But I do use small quantities of butter where I consider the flavour essential, and sometimes mix a little with vegetable oil for frying breadcrumbs or bread toppings.

Stocks and sauces also contribute to the flavour and interest of successful dishes. A good vegetable stock does not take long to make and may be frozen in small quantities for future use. However, when I'm in a hurry I make use of the excellent Hugli stock cubes from the health food store. Yeast extracts may be used to strengthen the flavour of stocks, and a little wine is delicious in stews and casseroles.

All important to the success of these dishes are the toppings — pastry, melted cheese or crunchy mixtures of nuts or breadcrumbs. Essentially, the topping should provide a contrast in texture, and sometimes it will also make the dish more substantial and lift it into the 'main course' category. Pastry made with wholemeal or 81 per cent extraction flour has lots of flavour, too, and makes a positive contribution to the food value of the dish with vitamins, minerals and cereal fibre. Because these flours are 'live', they deteriorate in storage — unlike the popular brands of white flour which keep forever because there's nothing left in them to go off. So use your flour while it is still fresh — it's a good idea, too, to pencil the date of purchase on the packet as a reminder. If you do need to store flour, wrap the packet in a plastic bag and pop it in the freezer.

Just as the flour will not keep for ever, made-up pastry dough will darken unpleasantly if kept in the fridge. If you want to make up a quantity of pastry for several days, take it to the 'rubbed in' stage and store the dry mix in the fridge, adding water when you come to cook. Similarly, it's best not to store uncooked pancake batter — simply make extra pancakes, wrap and chill them for use the following day.

The toppings I have given are interchangeable in many dishes. If you are in a hurry and just need a light lunch dish, substitute nuts or breadcrumbs for a pastry covering. A favourite casserole with a cheesy topping may be made more substantial and given a new look if you make it with dumplings for a change. But remember that dumplings do tend to absorb the sauce in a dish, so you may need to add a little more water or stock.

These recipes all give four average portions unless otherwise stated, but this should be taken as a guide only, depending on individual appetites and the way you like to build your family menus. The most useful recipes, I believe, are the ones which widen your cooking horizons and inspire you to carry on experimenting yourself. I hope that you will find many such ideas in the following pages!

1.

BASIC RECIPES: PASTRY, TOPPINGS AND SAUCES

SHORTCRUST PASTRY

Imperial (Metric)
½ lb (¼ kilo) plain 81% wholemeal flour
½ teaspoonful sea salt
4 oz (100g) polyunsaturated margarine
Cold water to mix

American
2 cupsful plain 81% wholewheat flour
½ teaspoonful sea salt
½ cupful polyunsaturated margarine
Cold water to mix

1. Mix flour and salt and rub in the fat until mixture resembles breadcrumbs.

2. Add about four tablespoonsful water and mix to a firm dough.

3. Wrap in clingfilm and leave in a cool place for 15-30 minutes before using.

Note: In recipes calling for a different amount of flour, follow the method, using the rest of the ingredients in proportion.

WHOLEMEAL PASTRY

Imperial (Metric)
½ lb (¼ kilo) wholemeal flour
1 teaspoonful sea salt
3 oz (75g) polyunsaturated
  margarine
Cold water to mix

American
2 cupsful wholewheat flour
1 teaspoonful sea salt
⅓ cupful polyunsaturated margarine
Cold water to mix

1. Sift the flour and salt, returning to the bowl any bran left in the sieve.

2. Rub the margarine in very lightly and finish mixing with a fork. Handle as little as possible.

3. Still using a fork, mix in just enough water to make a stiff dough. Gather the dough together with the hands, sprinkle with a little more flour and leave in a cool place for 15 minutes.

4. Roll out on a lightly floured surface, working as quickly as possible. If the weather is warm, roll the pastry out between two sheets of waxed or greaseproof paper. When possible, cut dough to fit pie plates, etc., then chill lightly in the fridge before baking.

Note: In recipes calling for a different amount of flour, follow method, using rest of ingredients in proportion.

FLAKY PASTRY

Imperial (Metric)	American
½ lb (¼ kilo) plain 81% wholemeal flour	2 cupsful plain 81% wholewheat flour
Pinch of sea salt	Pinch of sea salt
5-6 oz (125-150g) butter	½-¾ cupful butter
Ice cold water to mix	Ice cold water to mix

1. Mix flour and salt. Divide butter into three portions. Rub one portion into the flour in the usual way and mix to a stiff dough with a little cold water. Roll out into a rectangle.

2. Take the second portion of fat, cut it into small pieces and dot it over two-thirds of the dough. Dust with flour and fold the dough in three lengthways.

3. Turn the pastry at right angles and lightly indent it at intervals with the rolling pin (this helps to make it rise evenly). Seal the open ends.

4. Leave in a cool place for 1¼ hours, then roll out and repeat the process with the remaining fat.

5. Rest and roll the dough again, sealing the ends. If the paste becomes too soft and sticky, let it firm up in the fridge before rolling.

Note: In recipes calling for a different amount of flour, follow the method, using the rest of the ingredients in proportion.

QUICK 'FLAKY' PASTRY

Imperial (Metric)
½ lb (¼ kilo) plain 81% wholemeal
    flour
Pinch of sea salt
6 oz (150g) butter, well chilled
Ice cold water to mix

American
2 cupsful plain 81% wholewheat
    flour
Pinch of sea salt
¾ cupful butter, well chilled
Ice cold water to mix

1. Mix flour and salt. Make sure that butter is very hard (firm up in the freezer if necessary before use).

2. Using a coarse grater, grate the butter into the flour.

3. Mix in the butter with a fork. Add enough cold water to make a stiff dough, mixing with the fork to avoid handling.

4. Form quickly into a ball with floured hands and leave in a cool place for 15 minutes before rolling out.

Note: In recipes calling for a different amount of flour, follow the method, using the rest of the ingredients in proportion.

CHEESY CRUMB TOPPING

Imperial (Metric)	American
2 tablespoonsful dry wholemeal breadcrumbs	2 tablespoonsful dry wholewheat breadcrumbs
½ oz (15g) polyunsaturated margarine	1½ tablespoonsful polyunsaturated margarine
2 oz (50g) grated cheese	½ cupful grated cheese
1 tablespoonful chopped parsley	1 tablespoonful chopped parsley
Pinch of sea salt	Pinch of sea salt

1. Fry the breadcrumbs in the margarine over medium heat until crisp. Leave them to cool.

2. Stir in the cheese and parsley and season with salt.

3. Store in fridge in screw-topped jar if not for immediate use.

SOYA CRUMBLE TOPPING

Imperial (Metric)	American
3 oz (75g) plain 81% wholemeal flour	¾ cupful plain 81% wholewheat flour
1 oz (25g) toasted soya flakes	¼ cupful toasted soya flakes
¼ teaspoonful sea salt	¼ teaspoonful sea salt
1 teaspoonful baking powder	1 teaspoonful baking soda
1 oz (25g) polyunsaturated margarine	2½ tablespoonsful polyunsaturated margarine
1 oz (25g) grated cheese	2½ tablespoonsful grated cheese
Pinch of paprika	Pinch of paprika

1. Mix together the flour, toasted soya flakes, sea salt and baking powder. Rub in the margarine

2. Stir in the grated cheese and paprika to taste.

3. Sprinkle thickly over casseroles and cook according to recipe directions.

COBBLER TOPPING

Imperial (Metric)
½ lb (¼ kilo) self-raising 81%
  wholemeal flour
½ teaspoonful sea salt
2 oz (50g) polyunsaturated
  margarine
¼ pint (150ml) milk
3 oz (75g) grated cheese

American
2 cupsful self-raising 81%
  wholewheat flour
½ teaspoonful sea salt
¼ cupful polyunsaturated margarine
⅔ cupful milk
¾ cupful grated cheese

1. Mix the flour and sea salt and rub in the margarine with the fingertips until the mixture looks like fine breadcrumbs.

2. Add about three-quarters of the milk and work to a soft dough. The whole amount may not be necessary as flours vary in absorbency. The dough should not be too wet.

3. Roll out on a lightly floured surface to a rectangle about 9 in. (23cm) by 11 in. (28cm).

4. Sprinkle with the cheese and roll up from the longer side of the rectangle to make a long roll. Cut into 12 pieces.

5. Arrange the rounds on top of the casserole and cook according to recipe.

DUMPLINGS I

Imperial (Metric)	American
6 oz (150g) wholemeal flour	1½ cupsful wholewheat flour
3 teaspoonsful baking powder	3 teaspoonsful baking soda
Seasoning to taste	Seasoning to taste
1½ oz (40g) butter	2 tablespoonsful butter
1 medium egg	1 medium egg
3 tablespoonsful milk (approx.)	3 tablespoonsful milk (approx.)

1. Mix the flour and baking powder and season with sea salt and pepper. Rub in the butter.

2. Beat the egg with 2 tablespoonsful milk, and mix quickly with the flour to make a stiff dough, adding a little more milk if needed.

3. Roll the dough into small dumplings and cook according to recipe.

DUMPLINGS II

Imperial (Metric)	American
6 oz (150g) plain 81% wholemeal flour	1½ cupsful plain 81% wholewheat flour
½ teaspoonful sea salt	½ teaspoonful sea salt
1 teaspoonful baking powder	1 teaspoonful baking soda
3 oz (75g) polyunsaturated margarine	4 tablespoonsful polyunsaturated margarine
½ teaspoonful dried basil or tarragon	½ teaspoonful dried basil or tarragon

1. Mix the flour, sea salt and baking powder.

2. Rub in the margarine and add dried herbs.

3. Mix to a firm dough with a little water.

4. Form into small dumplings and cook according to recipe.

PANCAKES

Imperial (Metric)	American
4 oz (100g) plain 81% wholemeal flour	1 cupful plain 81% wholewheat flour
Pinch of sea salt	Pinch of sea salt
1 egg and 1 yolk	1 egg and 1 yolk
½ pint (¼ litre) milk	1⅓ cupsful milk
1 tablespoonful vegetable oil	1 tablespoonful vegetable oil

1. Mix the flour and sea salt. Make a well in the centre and add the egg and yolk.

2. Add a little milk and draw the flour in gradually, stirring well with a wooden spoon and adding more milk as necessary. Add the oil and the rest of the milk.

3. Beat the batter thoroughly and leave, covered, for two to three hours. Beat again before using and add a little cold water if the batter has thickened up too much.

4. Make pancakes in a 6 in. (15cm) pan, lightly oiled. Makes about 15 thin pancakes.

Note: If not for immediate use, refrigerate or freeze pancakes, separating them with small pieces of foil between the layers.

WHITE SAUCE

Imperial (Metric)	American
1 oz (25g) butter or polyunsaturated margarine	2½ tablespoonsful butter or polyunsaturated margarine
1 oz (25g) plain 81% wholemeal flour	¼ cupful plain 81% wholewheat flour
½ pint (275ml) milk or mixture of milk and vegetable water	1⅓ cupsful milk or mixture of milk and vegetable water
Seasoning to taste	Seasoning to taste

1. Melt the butter in a small pan. Remove from the heat and stir in the flour.

2. Cook over gentle heat for a few minutes, stirring.

3. Gradually blend in the milk, off the heat, stirring well to avoid lumps. Bring to the boil and simmer gently until thickened.

Note: In recipes calling for a different amount of white sauce, e.g. ¾ pint (275ml), follow sauce recipe using ¾ pint (275ml)/2 cupsful milk and other ingredients in proportion.

CHEESE SAUCE

Follow recipe for White Sauce.Stir in 2 oz (50g)/½ cupful grated cheese and a good pinch of dry mustard. A pinch of paprika may also be added if you wish.

FRUITY SAUCE

Imperial (Metric)	American
1 medium onion	1 medium onion
½ oz (15g) butter	1½ tablespoonsful butter
¼ pint (140ml) red wine	⅔ cupful red wine
1 bay leaf	1 bay leaf
Juice and rind of 2 oranges	Juice and rind of 2 oranges
Sea salt to taste	Sea salt to taste
1-2 teaspoonsful redcurrant jelly	1-2 teaspoonsful seedless redcurrant jelly
Mushroom ketchup to taste	Mushroom catsup to taste

1. Chop the onion roughly and fry gently in the butter until beginning to soften.

2. Add the wine and bay leaf and bring to the boil. Simmer until the wine is reduced by two-thirds. Add the orange juice and thinly peeled rind, bring back to the boil and simmer for 5 minutes.

3. Strain into a clean pan, add the redcurrant jelly to taste and stir over low heat to dissolve. Add 1-2 teaspoonsful mushroom ketchup and adjust seasoning.

Note: For a very thick sauce, reduce again after adding orange juice.

TANGY APPLE SAUCE

Imperial (Metric)	American
¾ lb (350g) cooking apples	12 ounces cooking apples
Light soft raw cane sugar to taste	Light soft raw cane sugar to taste
½ oz (15g) butter	1½ tablespoonsful butter
1 teaspoonful grated lemon rind	1 teaspoonful grated lemon rind
Lemon juice	Lemon juice
Mixed spice	Mixed spice

1. Peel, core and chop the apples. Cook them with just enough water to prevent sticking. When soft, mash well or rub through a sieve for a smoother sauce.

2. Add sugar to taste but do not make too sweet. Beat in the butter.

3. Add the grated lemon rind and a good squeeze of lemon juice.

4. Season to taste with mixed spice. Serve warm.

TOMATO SAUCE

Imperial (Metric)	American
1 small onion	1 small onion
1 clove garlic	1 clove garlic
1 tablespoonful vegetable oil	1 tablespoonful vegetable oil
14 oz (400g) tin tomatoes	1 medium can tomatoes
1 bay leaf	1 bay leaf
2-3 parsley stalks	2-3 parsley stalks
3-4 leaves fresh basil or	3-4 leaves fresh basil or
1 teaspoonful dried thyme or	1 teaspoonful dried thyme or
marjoram	marjoram
Seasoning to taste	Seasoning to taste
Dash of sherry or ½ glass white	Dash of sherry or ½ glass white
wine (optional)	wine (optional)

1. Peel and chop the onion. Peel and crush the garlic. Fry them gently together in the oil until beginning to soften.

2. Add the tomatoes and herbs and season with salt and pepper. Add sherry or wine.

3. Bring to the boil, lower the heat and simmer for about 20 minutes or until the sauce is thick. Remove the bay leaf and parsley stalks before serving.

Note: May be rubbed through a sieve for a smooth sauce if you prefer.

SPICY TOMATO SAUCE

Imperial (Metric)	American
1 small onion	1 small onion
1 clove garlic	1 clove garlic
1 tablespoonful vegetable oil	1 tablespoonful vegetable oil
14 oz (400g) tin tomatoes	1 medium can tomatoes
½ pint (275ml) water	1⅓ cupsful water
1 tablespoonful light soft raw cane sugar	1 tablespoonful light soft raw cane sugar
2 tablespoonsful wine or cider vinegar	2 tablespoonsful wine or cider vinegar
2 slices lemon	2 slices lemon
1 stick celery, roughly chopped	1 stalk celery, roughly chopped
1 teaspoonful chopped fresh basil or ½ teaspoonful dried basil	1 teaspoonful chopped fresh basil or ½ teaspoonful dried basil
2-3 sprigs parsley	2-3 sprigs parsley
2-3 sprigs thyme or marjoram or ½ teaspoonful dried marjoram	2-3 sprigs thyme or marjoram or ½ teaspoonful dried marjoram
Sea salt to taste	Sea salt to taste
1-2 tablespoonsful tomato *purée*	1-2 tablespoonsful tomato paste
Tabasco sauce to taste	Tabasco sauce to taste

1. Peel and chop the onion and garlic and fry gently in the oil until beginning to soften.

2. Add all remaining ingredients except the tomato *purée* and Tabasco, bring to the boil and simmer for 20-30 minutes, adding a little more water if the mixture thickens too much. Cool slightly.

3. Strain through a coarse sieve, rubbing through with a wooden spoon to extract as much pulp as possible from the vegetables.

4. Return the sauce to the pan, taste for seasoning and add the tomato *purée* and Tabasco. (For a very thick sauce, boil fast to reduce slightly before adding the final ingredients.) More lemon juice may be added to sharpen the flavour if you wish.

VEGETABLE STOCK

Imperial (Metric)	American
2 sticks celery, with leaves	2 stalks celery, with leaves
1 onion	1 onion
1 clove garlic	1 clove garlic
1 carrot	1 carrot
6 peppercorns	6 peppercorns
6 sprigs parsley, including coarse stalks	6 sprigs parsley, including coarse stalks
2-3 sprigs thyme or ½ teaspoonful dried thyme	2-3 sprigs thyme or ½ teaspoonful dried thyme
2-3 sprigs other fresh herbs as available or ½ teaspoonful dried herbs	2-3 sprigs other fresh herbs as available or ½ teaspoonful dried herbs
3 pints (1½ litres) water	7½ cupsful water

1. Wash the celery and break it up roughly. Peel and halve the onion and garlic. Scrape the carrot and cut it up roughly.

2. Put the vegetables and herbs into a large pan with the water, bring to the boil and simmer for about 45 minutes. Strain.

Note: For stronger flavoured stock, make as above, then boil the strained stock for about 30 minutes or until reduced by half. A little yeast extract may be added to the finished stock for extra flavour if you wish.

2.

CRISPY-TOPPED DISHES

SPICY AUBERGINE WITH LENTILS

Imperial (Metric)	American
1 lb (½ kilo) aubergine	1 pound eggplant
4 oz (100g) Continental lentils	½ cupful Continental lentils
Vegetable oil	Vegetable oil
1 large onion	1 large onion
1 clove garlic	1 clove garlic
2 teaspoonsful curry powder, or to taste	2 teaspoonsful curry powder, or to taste
4 teaspoonsful grated fresh ginger root, or to taste	4 teaspoonsful grated fresh ginger root, or to taste
2 tablespoonsful chopped fresh coriander or parsley	2 tablespoonsful chopped fresh cilantro or parsley
Seasoning to taste	Seasoning to taste
4 tablespoonsful tomato *purée*	4 tablespoonsful tomato paste
4 tablespoonsful natural yogurt	4 tablespoonsful natural yogurt
3-4 tablespoonsful dry wholemeal breadcrumbs	3-4 tablespoonsful dry wholewheat breadcrumbs
1 oz (25g) butter or polyunsaturated margarine	2½ tablespoonsful butter or polyunsaturated margarine

1. Peel the aubergine (eggplant), slice, sprinkle with salt and leave for 30 minutes. Rinse, drain and dry on paper towelling. Fry the slices quickly in about 1 in. (2½cm) vegetable oil until almost soft, turning to brown both sides. Drain well on paper towelling.

2. Peel and chop the onion and garlic. Heat a little oil in a large
    pan and fry the onion, garlic and curry powder over medium heat
    until the onion is transparent. Add grated ginger and coriander
    (cilantro) or parsley and fry for a further 2-3 minutes.

3. Stir in the tomato *purée*. Chop the cooked aubergine (eggplant)
    and add to the tomato-onion mixture.

4. Transfer to a greased ovenproof dish and cook, covered, for about
    20 minutes at 350°F/180°C (Gas Mark 4). Remove from the oven
    and allow to cool slightly. Meanwhile, fry the breadcrumbs in
    butter until crisp.

5. Stir the yogurt into the vegetable mixture and top with the fried
    crumbs. Serve warm.

AUBERGINE ITALIAN STYLE

Imperial (Metric)
1½ lb (¾ kilo) aubergine
Vegetable oil
14 oz (400g) tin tomatoes
Seasoning to taste
½ lb (¼ kilo) Cheddar cheese,
   grated
1 teaspoonful dried oregano
1 teaspoonful chopped fresh basil
   or ½ teaspoonful dried basil
Cheesy Crumb Topping (page 17)

American
1½ pounds eggplant
Vegetable oil
1 medium can tomatoes
Seasoning to taste
2 cupsful grated cheese
1 teaspoonful dried oregano
1 teaspoonful chopped fresh basil
   or ½ teaspoonful dried basil
Cheesy Crumb Topping (page 17)

1. Peel the aubergine (eggplant) and cut into ½ in. (1cm) slices. Sprinkle well with salt and leave for at least 30 minutes.

2. Wash the aubergine (eggplant) slices well under running water, drain and pat dry on paper towelling. Fry the slices in a large frying pan in about 1 in. (2½cm) oil, using a fairly high heat so that they do not absorb the oil. Fry a few slices at a time, turning once to brown both sides, and drain well on paper towelling.

3. Drain the tomatoes and chop roughly. Butter an ovenproof casserole.

4. Make layers of aubergine (eggplant) and tomatoes, sprinkling with the grated cheese, herbs, salt and pepper. The top layer should be aubergine (eggplant) slices.

5. Cover with the cheese topping and bake at 400°F/200°C (Gas Mark 6) for about 30 minutes.

AFRICAN EGG AND PEPPER BAKE

Imperial (Metric)	American
4 tablespoonsful dry wholemeal breadcrumbs	4 tablespoonsful dry wholewheat breadcrumbs
5 oz (125g) butter or polyunsaturated margarine	2/3 cupful butter or polyunsaturated margarine
2 large onions	2 large onions
3 cloves garlic	3 cloves garlic
2 large green peppers	2 large green peppers
4 tomatoes, or equivalent in canned tomatoes	4 tomatoes, or equivalent in canned tomatoes
Seasoning to taste	Seasoning to taste
Tabasco sauce	Tabasco sauce
4 eggs	4 eggs

1. Fry the breadcrumbs until crisp in 1 oz (25g) butter or margarine.

2. Peel the onions and slice thinly. Peel and chop the garlic. Fry together in half the remaining butter or margarine until soft and beginning to brown. Remove with slotted spoon and reserve.

3. De-seed the peppers and cut them into thin strips. Peel and chop the tomatoes.

4. Fry the peppers, adding remaining butter to the pan as needed. When they are beginning to soften, add the chopped tomatoes. Cook together for 5 minutes, then turn up heat and cook, stirring well, until pan liquid is well reduced.

5. Return the onion and garlic to the pan and mix well. Season with salt and pepper and Tabasco to taste. The mixture should be well spiced.

6. Turn the mixture into a small, shallow ovenproof dish. Make 4 depressions in the vegetables and break an egg into each.

7. Sprinkle with the fried crumbs and bake at 300°F/150°C (Gas Mark 2) for about 20 minutes or until the egg whites are just set.

Note: Serves 4 as starter, 2 as main course.

MEXICAN CORN

Imperial (Metric)	American
1 medium onion	1 medium onion
1 clove garlic	1 clove garlic
Vegetable oil	Vegetable oil
½ lb (¼ kilo) courgettes	8 ounces zucchini
1 green pepper	1 green pepper
3 fresh corn cobs or 10 oz (275g) can sweet corn	3 fresh corn cobs or 1 medium can sweet corn
¾ lb (350g) tomatoes or 14 oz (400g) tin tomatoes	12 ounces tomatoes or 1 medium can tomatoes
1 teaspoonful chilli powder, or to taste	1 teaspoonful chili powder, or to taste
Seasoning to taste	Seasoning to taste
Butter or polyunsaturated margarine	Butter or polyunsaturated margarine
Cheesy Crumb Topping (page 17)	Cheesy Crumb Topping (page 17)

1. Peel and chop the onion and garlic and fry gently in a little oil until soft.

2. Wash and dry the courgettes (zucchini) and cut into thin rounds. Remove seeds and membranes from the green pepper and cut into thin strips. Add the courgettes (zucchini) and peppers to the pan with the onion and fry briskly for 3-4 minutes, adding more oil if necessary.

3. If using fresh corn, scrape the kernels from the cobs and blanch them in boiling salted water for 5 minutes. If using canned corn, drain it well.

4. Skin and chop the tomatoes. If using tinned tomatoes, drain and chop. Mix the corn and tomatoes with the courgette (zucchini) and pepper mixture and season with chilli powder, salt and pepper.

5. Transfer to a greased pie dish, sprinkle with the topping and bake at 350°F/180°C (Gas Mark 4) for 30 minutes.

BRUSSELS SPROUT AND ALMOND CASSEROLE

Imperial (Metric)	American
1½ lb (¾ kilo) brussels sprouts	1½ pounds brussels sprouts
2 oz (50g) butter	¼ cupful butter
1 large onion, finely chopped	1 large onion, finely chopped
3-4 sticks celery, finely chopped	3-4 stalks celery, finely chopped
3 heaped tablespoonsful plain 81% wholemeal flour	3 heaped tablespoonsful plain 81% wholewheat flour
Scant ¾ pint (400ml) milk	Scant 2 cupsful milk
½ teaspoonful grated nutmeg	½ teaspoonful grated nutmeg
½ teaspoonful paprika	½ teaspoonful paprika
Seasoning to taste	Seasoning to taste
4 oz (100g) cheese, diced	1½ cupsful diced cheese
3 tablespoonsful chopped, blanched almonds	3 tablespoonsful chopped, blanched almonds
4 tablespoonsful Cheesy Crumb Topping (page 17)	4 tablespoonsful Cheesy Crumb Topping (page 17)
1 oz (25g) butter or polyunsaturated margarine	2½ tablespoonsful butter or polyunsaturated margarine

1. Trim the sprouts and cook in boiling salted water for 5 minutes. Drain and cut into pieces if large.

2. Melt the butter in a saucepan and fry the chopped onion gently until beginning to soften. Stir in the chopped celery and cook for 5 minutes.

3. Stir in the flour and cook for 3-4 minutes. Remove pan from the heat and stir the milk in gradually. Cook, still stirring, until thickened.

4. Add nutmeg and paprika and season to taste with salt and pepper. Mix in the sprouts and cheese.

5. Spoon the mixture into a greased casserole and sprinkle with chopped almonds and Cheesy Crumb Topping.

6. Dot with butter and bake at 375°F/190°C (Gas Mark 5) for 20-30 minutes.

SPICY BROCCOLI CRUMBLE

Imperial (Metric)	American
4 eggs	4 eggs
1 medium onion	1 medium onion
1 clove garlic	1 clove garlic
2 oz (50g) butter or polyunsaturated margarine	¼ cupful butter or polyunsaturated margarine
1 dessertspoonful curry powder or to taste	2 teaspoonsful curry powder or to taste
2 tablespoonsful wholemeal flour	2 tablespoonsful wholewheat flour
⅔ pint (350ml) milk	1½ cupsful milk
Seasoning to taste	Seasoning to taste
1 lb (½ kilo) broccoli	1 pound broccoli
Soya Crumble Topping (page 18) or Cheesy Crumb Topping (page 17)	Soya Crumble Topping (page 18) or Cheesy Crumb Topping (page 17)

1. Hard-boil the eggs, crack their shells and cool under running water.

2. Peel and chop the onion and garlic and fry in the butter with the curry powder over medium heat until beginning to brown.

3. Add the flour and milk to make a thick sauce (for method, see White Sauce, page 23). Season to taste.

4. Cook the broccoli in boiling salted water until tender but still firm and drain well. Place in a greased ovenproof dish. Halve the hard boiled eggs and arrange over the broccoli.

5. Spoon the sauce over the eggs and sprinkle with the topping.

6. Bake at 375°F/190°C (Gas Mark 5) for about 20 minutes.

NUT BAKE WITH CRUMBLE TOPPING

Imperial (Metric)	American
1 onion	1 onion
1 clove garlic	1 clove garlic
4 oz (100g) mushrooms	2 cupsful mushrooms
3 oz (75g) polyunsaturated margarine	1/2 cupful polyunsaturated margarine
3 heaped tablespoonsful fine or medium oatmeal	3 heaped tablespoonsful fine or medium oatmeal
4 oz (100g) mixed nuts, milled or finely chopped	3/4 cupful milled or chopped mixed nuts
1/2 pint (1/4 litre) milk	1 1/3 cupsful milk
1 teaspoonful mixed dried herbs	1 teaspoonful mixed dried herbs
1 egg	1 egg
Seasoning to taste	Seasoning to taste
Soya Crumble Topping (page 18)	Soya Crumble Topping (page 18)

1. Peel and chop the onion and garlic. Wash, dry and chop the mushrooms.

2. Melt the margarine in a large pan and cook the onion, garlic and mushrooms gently until beginning to soften.

3. Gradually add the oatmeal, nuts, herbs and milk and mix well. Cool slightly.

4. Beat the egg and stir in. Season well with salt and pepper.

5. Turn into a greased pie dish and bake for 30 minutes at 350°F/180°C (Gas Mark 4).

6. Remove from the oven and sprinkle with the crumble topping. Return to the oven and bake for a further 15 minutes.

RICE AND OKRA BAKE

Imperial (Metric)	American
¾ lb (350g) fresh okra	12 ounces fresh okra
1 small green pepper	1 small green pepper
1 large onion	1 large onion
1 clove garlic	1 clove garlic
Vegetable oil	Vegetable oil
14 oz (400g) tin tomatoes	1 medium can tomatoes
1½ oz (40g) butter	4 tablespoonsful butter
4 oz (100g) cooked long-grain brown rice	⅔ cupful cooked long-grain brown rice
4 oz (100g) grated cheese	1 cupful grated cheese
Seasoning to taste	Seasoning to taste
1 teaspoonful dried basil	1 teaspoonful dried basil
3-4 tablespoonsful dry wholemeal breadcrumbs	3-4 tablespoonsful dry wholewheat breadcrumbs

1. Top and tail the okra and cut each into 2-3 pieces if large. Remove seeds and membranes from the pepper and cut pepper into small strips.

2. Peel and chop the onion and garlic and fry gently in a little oil until beginning to soften.

3. Butter a deep ovenproof dish. Make layers of the okra, tomatoes, onion, pepper, rice and cheese, seasoning with salt, pepper and basil between the layers and finishing with a layer of cheese. Pour in the juice from the tomatoes.

4. Cover with foil and bake at 350°F/180°C (Gas Mark 4) for 1 hour or until okra is soft.

5. Fry the breadcrumbs in the remaining butter and sprinkle over the dish before serving.

MUSHROOM AND ALMOND RICE BAKE

Imperial (Metric)	American
1 medium onion	1 medium onion
½ lb (¼ kilo) long-grain brown rice	1 cupful long-grain brown rice
Vegetable oil	Vegetable oil
1 pint (½ litre) vegetable stock· (page 29)	2½ cupsful vegetable stock (page 29)
3 × 1 in. (2cm) strips orange peel	3 × 1 in. strips orange peel
Seasoning to taste	Seasoning to taste
Dash of sherry (optional)	Dash of sherry (optional)
2 oz (50g) blanched almonds	½ cupful blanched almonds
4 oz (100g) mushrooms	2 cupsful mushrooms
1 oz (25g) butter	2½ tablespoonsful butter
Cheesy Crumb Topping (page 17)	Cheesy Crumb Topping (page 17)
2-3 tablespoonsful chopped parsley	2-3 tablespoonsful chopped parsley

1. Peel the onion and chop finely. Wash the rice and dry thoroughly.

2. Using a fireproof casserole with lid, fry the onion in a little oil, uncovered, until beginning to soften. Add the dry rice and fry, turning with a wooden spoon, until the grains deepen in colour and are well coated with oil.

3. Add about two-thirds of the stock and season with salt and pepper. Add the strips of thinly peeled orange rind.

4. Cover and bake at 350°F/180°C (Gas Mark 4) for about 1¼ hours, adding more stock as needed during cooking.

5. When the rice is soft and the stock nearly all absorbed, chop the almonds, slice the mushrooms and fry in butter until the mushrooms are soft. Stir into the rice.

6. Sprinkle the topping over the casserole and bake uncovered for a further 15 minutes or until well browned. Sprinkle with chopped parsley before serving.

RICE AND MIXED VEGETABLE CASSEROLE

Imperial (Metric)	American
2 tablespoonsful long-grain brown rice	2 tablespoonsful long-grain brown rice
2 tomatoes	2 tomatoes
2 small courgettes	2 small zucchini
1 large onion	1 large onion
2 medium potatoes	2 medium potatoes
1 green pepper	1 green pepper
2 oz (50g) butter	¼ cupful butter
Seasoning to taste	Seasoning to taste
Dried marjoram	Dried marjoram
Dried tarragon	Dried tarragon
2-3 tablespoonsful vegetable stock (page 29)	2-3 tablespoonsful vegetable stock (page 29)
3 tablespoonsful thin cream or top milk	2-3 tablespoonsful light cream
Cheesy Crumb Topping (page 17)	Cheesy Crumb Topping (page 17)

1. Cook the rice in boiling salted water until beginning to soften. Drain well and reserve.

2. Slice the tomatoes. Top and tail the courgettes (zucchini) and slice thinly. Peel the onion and potatoes and slice thinly. De-seed the pepper and cut it into thin strips.

3. Butter a deep pie dish and arrange half the tomato slices in the bottom. Season well with salt, pepper and marjoram. Place half the courgette (zucchini) slices over the tomatoes, then half the onion slices. Season with salt, pepper and tarragon.

4. Melt the remaining butter and spoon 1 tablespoonful over the vegetables. Add half the potato slices, season with salt, pepper and herbs and then add half the green pepper slices. Season and add 1 tablespoonful melted butter. Spoon on the cooked rice.

5. Repeat the layers of vegetables and seasoning, finishing with tomatoes. Moisten with stock and cover tightly with foil.

6. Bake at 350°F/180°C (Gas Mark 4) for 1½ hours. Remove the foil, pour the cream over and sprinkle with the topping. Bake for a further 15 minutes.

CREAMED POTATOES AND CARROTS AU GRATIN

Imperial (Metric)
1 lb (½ kilo) potatoes
½ lb (¼ kilo) carrots
4 oz (100g) butter or
   polyunsaturated margarine
1 medium onion, peeled and
   chopped
½ medium green pepper, seeded
   and chopped
2 tablespoonsful plain 81%
   wholemeal flour
¾ pint (400ml) milk
Seasoning to taste
6 oz (150g) grated cheese
Dash of Tabasco sauce
3 tablespoonsful dry wholemeal
   breadcrumbs
1 oz (25g) walnuts, chopped

American
1 pound potatoes
8 ounces carrots
½ cupful butter or polyunsaturated
   margarine
1 medium onion, peeled and
   chopped
½ medium green pepper, seeded
   and chopped
2 tablespoonsful plain 81%
   wholewheat flour
2 cupsful milk
Seasoning to taste
1½ cupsful grated cheese
Dash of Tabasco sauce
3 tablespoonsful dry wholewheat
   breadcrumbs
¼ cupful chopped English walnuts

1. Cook the potatoes in boiling salted water until just tender. Cool, peel and dice.

2. Scrape the carrots and slice very thinly. Fry in half the butter until beginning to soften, stirring occasionally. Remove with a draining spoon and reserve.

3. Add half the remaining butter to the pan and fry the onion and pepper until soft and beginning to colour. Remove from the heat and stir in the flour. Cook, still stirring, for 3-4 minutes.

4. Heat the milk and add to the onion and pepper mixture, off the heat, stirring well. Cook gently, still stirring, until thick.

5. Add seasoning and half the grated cheese. Stir until the cheese has melted. Add Tabasco to taste.

6. Butter a pie dish and make alternate layers of potatoes and carrots. Pour the sauce over and sprinkle with the remaining cheese.

7. Bake at 350°F/180°C (Gas Mark 4) for 30 minutes. Meanwhile, fry the breadcrumbs and walnuts in the remaining butter. Sprinkle over the dish before serving.

POTATO NUT CASSEROLE

Imperial (Metric)	American
1¹/₂ lb (³/₄ kilo) potatoes	1¹/₂ pounds potatoes
1 egg	1 egg
4 oz (100g) mushrooms, sliced	1¹/₂ cupsful sliced mushrooms
1 medium onion, chopped	1 medium onion, chopped
Vegetable oil	Vegetable oil
2 oz (50g) mixed walnuts and almonds, chopped	¹/₂ cupful chopped mixed English walnuts and almonds
2 oz (50g) soft wholemeal breadcrumbs	1 cupful soft wholewheat breadcrumbs
Seasoning to taste	Seasoning to taste
1 tablespoonful chopped parsley	1 tablespoonful chopped parsley
¹/₂ teaspoooonful dried basil	¹/₂ teaspoonful dried basil
¹/₄ teaspoonful dried marjoram	¹/₂ teaspoonful dried marjoram
2 oz (50g) butter, melted	¹/₄ cupful butter, melted
3 tablespoonsful vegetable stock (page 29)	3 tablespoonsful vegetable stock (page 29)
Cheesy Crumb Topping (page 17)	Cheesey Crumb Topping (page 17)

1. Cook the potatoes in boiling salted water until just tender. Do not over cook. Drain, then slice thinly. While the potatoes are cooking, hard-boil the egg, cool and reserve.

2. Heat a little oil in a frying pan and cook the mushrooms and onion gently until onion begins to soften. Transfer to a bowl and add the hard-boiled egg, mashed or sieved, the chopped nuts and breadcrumbs, salt, pepper and herbs.

3. Brush a casserole with melted butter and arrange the potatoes and the nut mixture in it in layers, adding a little melted butter to each layer and finishing with potatoes. Add the stock.

4. Sprinkle with the Cheesy Crumb Topping and bake at 375°F/190°C (Gas Mark 5) for 30 minutes.

LEEK, MUSHROOM AND CHESTNUT CASSEROLE

Imperial (Metric)
1 lb (½ kilo) chestnuts
4 leeks
¾ lb (350g) mushrooms
Vegetable oil
Seasoning to taste
¾ pint (400ml) White Sauce
   (page 23)
4-5 tablespoonsful dry wholemeal
   breadcrumbs
1 oz (25g) butter or polyunsaturated
   margarine

American
1 pound chestnuts
4 leeks
6 cupsful mushrooms
Vegetable oil
Seasoning to taste
2 cupsful White Sauce (page 23)
4-5 tablespoonsful dry wholewheat
   breadcrumbs
2½ tablespoonsful butter or
   polyunsaturated margarine

1. Peel the chestnuts and simmer in water until just soft. Drain and reserve.

2. While the chestnuts are cooking, split the leeks, cut into short lengths and wash thoroughly. Drain and dry. Wipe and slice the mushrooms, then fry them in a little oil until soft. Lift out with a draining spoon and fry the leeks until soft.

3. Make the White Sauce, which should be well thickened but not too stiff.

4. Mix the chestnuts with the leeks and mushrooms and transfer to a shallow ovenproof dish. Cover with the White Sauce.

5. Cover with foil and bake at 350°F/180°C (Gas Mark 4) for 20 minutes.

6. Fry the breadcrumbs in butter or margarine until crisp. Uncover the casserole, sprinkle with the breadcrumbs and return to the oven for a further 10 minutes.

GREEN BEAN AND TOMATO CASSEROLE

Imperial (Metric)	American
1 lb (½ kilo) French or runner beans	1 pound snap beans or green beans
4 large tomatoes	4 large tomatoes
Seasoning to taste	Seasoning to taste
Spicy Tomato Sauce (page 28)	Spicy Tomato Sauce (page 28)
4 oz (100g) cheese, grated	1 cupful grated cheese
Cheesy Crumb Topping (page 17)	Cheesy Crumb Topping (page 17)

1. If using French (snap) beans, top and tail them and break into halves. String the runner (green) beans and slice. Cook briefly in boiling salted water until just beginning to soften. Drain well.

2. Slice the tomatoes.

3. Place a layer of beans in a greased casserole and season lightly. Cover with tomato slices and repeat the layers, finishing with tomatoes.

4. Pour in enough Spicy Tomato Sauce to come two-thirds up the sides of the vegetables. Cover with Cheesy Crumb Topping.

5. Bake at 350°F/180°C (Gas Mark 4) for about 25 minutes or until top is well browned.

COURGETTE AND TOMATO CASSEROLE

Imperial (Metric)	American
1½ lb (¾ kilo) courgettes	1½ pounds zucchini
1½ lb (¾ kilo) tomatoes	1½ pounds tomatoes
1 large onion	1 large onion
1 clove garlic	1 clove garlic
3 oz (75g) butter	½ cupful butter
Seasoning to taste	Seasoning to taste
1 tablespoonful chopped parsley	2 teaspoonsful chopped parsley
½ teaspoonful dried basil	½ teaspoonful dried basil
4 oz (100g) grated cheese	1 cupful grated cheese
Cheesy Crumb Topping (page 17) or	Cheesy Crumb Topping (page 17) or
Cobbler Topping (page 19)	Cobbler Topping (page 19)

1. Wash courgettes (zucchini) and cut into fairly thin, even slices. Slice the tomatoes. Peel and chop the onion and garlic.

2. Cook the onion and garlic gently in the butter until soft and beginning to brown. Add the courgettes (zucchini) and cook, stirring occasionally, until they begin to soften. Cover the pan for part of the time to speed the process.

3. Arrange alternate layers of courgettes (zucchini) and tomatoes in an ovenproof dish. Season between the layers and sprinkle with herbs and cheese.

4. If using Cheesy Crumb Topping, cover the casserole lightly with foil and cook in the oven at 400°F/200°C (Gas Mark 6) for 25-30 minutes. Remove the foil, sprinkle the casserole with the topping and replace in the oven for 10-15 minutes.

5. If using Cobbler Topping for a more substantial dish, arrange the rounds on top of the casserole, bake at 400°F/200°C (Gas Mark 6) for about 25 minutes, then lower heat to 350°F/180°C (Gas Mark 4) for a further 10-15 minutes.

SOYA BEAN CASSEROLE

Imperial (Metric)	American
6 oz (150g) soya beans, soaked overnight	1 cupful soya beans, soaked overnight
1 medium onion	1 medium onion
2 cloves garlic	2 cloves garlic
4 tomatoes	4 tomatoes
2 leeks	2 leeks
2 carrots	2 carrots
Vegetable oil	Vegetable oil
3 tablespoonsful chopped parsley	3 tablespoonsful chopped parsley
1 teaspoonful dill seed	1 teaspoonful dill seed
2 tablespoonsful tomato *purée*	2 tablespoonsful tomato paste
Seasoning to taste	Seasoning to taste
3 tablespoonsful wholemeal breadcrumbs	3 tablespoonsful wholewheat breadcrumbs
1 oz (25g) butter or polyunsaturated margarine	2½ tablespoonsful butter or polyunsaturated margarine
1 oz (25g) grated Parmesan cheese	¼ cupful grated Parmesan cheese

1. Rinse the soaked beans in cold water, drain, cover with fresh water, bring to the boil and simmer for 2 hours or until soft. Drain, reserving ½ pint (1⅓ cupsful) cooking liquid.

2. Peel and chop the onion, peel and crush the garlic. Slice the tomatoes. Trim the leeks, wash well, dry and slice. Clean the carrots and chop finely.

3. Fry the onion and garlic in a little oil until beginning to soften. Add the leeks and carrots and fry briskly for 10 minutes, stirring frequently.

4. Mix in the cooked beans, add 2 tablespoonsful parsley and the dill seeds. Mix tomato *purée* with the reserved cooking liquid from the beans and add to the mixture. Season with salt and pepper.

5. Transfer to a casserole, arrange the tomato slices on top, sprinkle with basil and the remaining parsley. Season lightly.

6. Top with the breadcrumbs, dot with butter and sprinkle with the grated cheese.

7. Bake at 375°F/190°C (Gas Mark 5) for 40 minutes.

CRISP-TOP TOFU CASSEROLE

Imperial (Metric)

1 medium onion
2 cloves garlic
Vegetable oil
4 oz (100g) carrots
½ lb (¼ kilo) courgettes
¼ pint (140ml) white wine
¼ pint (130ml) vegetable stock (page 29)
4 oz (100g) cooked long-grain brown rice (cooked weight)
1 dessertspoonful chopped fresh coriander
1 tablespoonful grated fresh ginger root
½ teaspoonful curry powder
Pinch ground cinnamon
Pinch ground nutmeg
Seasoning to taste
1 tablespoonful tomato *purée*
4 oz (100g) millet
10 oz (275g) tofu
Cheesy Crumb Topping (Page 17)

American

1 medium onion
2 cloves garlic
Vegetable oil
4 ounces carrots
8 ounces zucchini
⅔ cupful white wine
⅔ cupful vegetable stock (page 29)
⅔ cupful cooked long-grain brown rice
2 teaspoonsful chopped cilantro
1 tablespoonful grated fresh ginger root
½ teaspoonful curry powder
Pinch ground cinnamon
Pinch ground nutmeg
Seasoning to taste
1 tablespoonful tomato paste
½ cupful millet
1⅔ cupsful tofu
Cheesy Crumb Topping (Page 17)

1. Peel and chop the onion and garlic and fry in vegetable oil until beginning to soften.

2. Scrape the carrots and slice thinly. Wash, dry and slice the courgettes (zucchini), then add them with the carrots to the pan and fry briskly for 4-5 minutes.

3. Pour in the wine and stock. Add the cooked rice, herbs, spices and seasonings and the tomato *purée*.

4. Cover and cook in the oven at 350°F/180°C (Gas Mark 4) for about 30 minutes or until the carrot is soft.

5. Meanwhile, brown the millet well in a little oil, add just under ½ pint (275ml) water and a good pinch of salt. Bring to the boil and simmer, uncovered, for about 20 minutes, stirring occasionally, until the millet is soft and most of the water has been absorbed.

6. Drain the tofu and cut into chunks. Stir the millet into the casserole and fold the tofu in carefully so that it does not break up. Replace the casserole in the oven for 15 minutes, adding a little more stock if necessary.

7. Sprinkle the topping over the casserole and brown under the grill.

LENTIL PIE

Imperial (Metric)	American
½ lb (¼ kilo) lentils	1 cupful lentils
1 onion	1 onion
¾ lb (350g) potatoes	12 ounces potatoes
2 tablespoonsful chopped parsley	2 tablespoonsful chopped parsley
Seasoning to taste	Seasoning to taste
2 tablespoonsful tomato *purée*	2 tablespoonsful tomato paste
Dash of Tabasco	Dash of Tabasco
Cheesy Crumb Topping (Page 17)	Cheesy Crumb Topping (Page 17)
1 oz (25g) butter	2½ tablespoonsful butter

1. Wash the lentils. Peel and slice the onion. Cook together in water to cover until the lentils are soft and the water absorbed. Cool and rub through a sieve.

2. While the lentils are cooking, peel the potatoes and cook in boiling salted water. Drain well and mash.

3. Mix the potatoes with the sieved lentils, parsley, seasoning to taste, tomato *purée* and Tabasco.

4. Transfer to a greased casserole, sprinkle with the topping, dot with butter and bake at 350°F/180°C (Gas Mark 4) for 20-30 minutes.

CHEESE AND MUSHROOM SUPPER

Imperial (Metric)	American
5 slices slightly dry wholemeal bread	5 slices slightly dry wholewheat bread
1 stick celery	1 stalk celery
1 medium onion	1 medium onion
1½ oz (40g) butter	4 tablespoonsful butter
6 oz (150g) mushrooms	3 cupsful mushrooms
6 oz (150g) cheese, coarsely grated	1½ cupsful grated cheese
2 eggs	2 eggs
1 pint (½ litre) milk	2½ cupsful milk
1 teaspoonful mixed dried herbs	1 teaspoonful mixed dried herbs
Seasoning to taste	Seasoning to taste
1 teaspoonful dry mustard	1 teaspoonful dry mustard
2 tablespoonsful mixed chopped nuts and wholemeal breadcrumbs	2 tablespoonsful mixed chopped nuts and wholewheat breadcrumbs

1. Cut the crusts from the bread. Cut the bread into 1 in. (2½cm) squares.

2. Scrub and chop the celery, peel and chop the onion. Fry in 1 oz (25g) butter until tender. Slice the mushrooms and add to the pan. Raise the heat and fry the vegetables briskly, stirring well, until the mushrooms are just cooked.

3. Grease a casserole or pie dish with the remaining butter and fill with layers of the bread, mushroom mixture and cheese, finishing with bread.

4. Beat the eggs with the milk, herbs, seasoning and mustard. Pour over the bread and leave to stand for 10 minutes.

5. Bake at 350°F/180°C (Gas Mark 4) for 35 minutes or until lightly set and browned. Sprinkle with the mixed nuts and breadcrumbs and replace in the oven for a further 10 minutes.

SPINACH AND SWEETCORN BAKE

Imperial (Metric)	American
1 lb (½ kilo) spinach	1 pound spinach
Seasoning to taste	Seasoning to taste
10 oz (275g) tin sweetcorn	1⅔ cupsful canned sweetcorn
¼ pint (150ml) milk	⅔ cupful milk
1 oz (25g) butter or polyunsaturated margarine	2½ tablespoonsful butter or polyunsaturated margarine
1 oz (25g) plain 81% wholemeal flour	¼ cupful plain 81% wholewheat flour
Paprika to taste	Paprika to taste
12 × 6in. (15cm) Pancakes (page 22)	12 × 6in. Crepes (page 22)
½ pint (¼ litre) Cheese Sauce (page 24)	1⅔ cupsful Cheese Sauce (page 24)
1 oz (25g) butter	2½ tablespoonsful butter
4 tablespoonsful dry wholemeal breadcrumbs	4 tablespoonsful dry wholewheat breadcrumbs
1 oz (25g) chopped walnuts	¼ cupful chopped English walnuts

1. Wash the spinach thoroughly and cook in the water clinging to the leaves. Drain, pressing out as much water as possible. Chop roughly and season to taste.

2. Drain the sweetcorn, reserving the liquid. Mix liquid with the milk to make ½ pint (275ml). Make into a white sauce with the butter and flour (for method see page 23). Season with salt, pepper and paprika.

3. Make the cheese sauce.

4. Arrange two pancakes overlapping in a shallow ovenproof dish. Spread them with some of the cooked spinach and top with 3-4 tablespoonsful cheese sauce. Cover with two more pancakes, top with sweetcorn and white sauce. Repeat layers until the vegetables and pancakes are used up, finishing with pancakes spread with cheese sauce.

5. Cover with foil and bake at 375°F/190°C (Gas Mark 5) for about 30 minutes or until hot and bubbling.

6. Melt the butter and fry the breadcrumbs until crisp. Mix with the chopped walnuts and sprinkle over the pancakes. Cut into wedges to serve.

YOGURT FLORENTINE BAKE

Imperial (Metric)	American
2 lb (1 kilo) fresh spinach	2 pounds fresh spinach
3 tablespoonsful natural yogurt	3 tablespoonsful natural yogurt
2 eggs	2 eggs
3 oz (75g) strongly flavoured cheese, grated	¾ cupful strongly flavoured cheese, grated
3 oz (75g) plain 81% wholemeal flour	¾ cupful plain 81% wholewheat flour
2 tablespoonsful vegetable oil	2 tablespoonsful vegetable oil
Seasoning	Seasoning
Cheesy Crumb Topping (Page 17) or sesame seeds	Cheesy Crumb Topping (Page 17) or sesame seeds

1. Wash the spinach well under cold running water to remove all grit.

2. Shake the leaves and cook in a large saucepan, covered, using just the water clinging to the leaves. Cool, drain well and chop finely.

3. Beat the yogurt with the eggs and mix in the grated cheese, flour, oil and cooked spinach. Add seasoning to taste.

4. Transfer the mixture to an oiled ovenproof dish, sprinkle with the topping or sesame seeds and bake at 350°F/180°C (Gas Mark 4) for 40 minutes.

CARAWAY ONION BAKE

Imperial (Metric)	American
1 lb (½ kilo) potatoes	1 pound potatoes
2 medium onions	2 medium onions
1 clove garlic	1 clove garlic
1 oz (25g) butter	2½ tablespoonsful butter
1 egg, plus 1 yolk	1 egg, plus 1 yolk
¼ pint (150ml) soured cream	⅔ cupful soured cream
Seasoning to taste	Seasoning to taste
½ teaspoonful caraway seeds	½ teaspoonful caraway seeds
2-3 tablespoonsful dry wholemeal breadcrumbs	2-3 tablespoonsful dry wholewheat breadcrumbs

1. Peel the potatoes and slice very thinly. Crush the garlic and rub round the inside of a pie dish. Butter the dish well, using about half the butter.

2. Peel the onions and slice thinly. Arrange the potatoes and onions in the dish in layers. Beat the egg and yolk, mix with the soured cream and season well with salt, pepper and caraway seeds. Pour evenly over the potatoes and onions.

3. Cover with a sheet of buttered foil and bake at 350°F/180°C (Gas Mark 4) for 1 hour 15 minutes or until the onions and potatoes are soft.

4. Fry the breadcrumbs in the remaining butter until crisp. Uncover the pie dish and sprinkle crumbs over the potatoes and onions before serving.

CHEESY TOPPED TOMATOES

Imperial (Metric)	American
8 tomatoes	8 tomatoes
2 oz (50g) wholemeal breadcrumbs	1 cupful wholewheat breadcrumbs
½ oz (15g) butter	1½ tablespoonsful butter
¼ pint (150ml) milk	⅔ cupful milk
2 oz (50g) grated cheese	½ cupful grated cheese
2 eggs	2 eggs
Seasoning to taste	Seasoning to taste
Cheesy Crumb Topping (Page 17)	Cheesy Crumb Topping (Page 17)

1. Drop the tomatoes into boiling water for a few seconds or sear by holding on a fork in a gas flame. Peel off the skins. Arrange the tomatoes in a shallow ovenproof dish.

2. Place the breadcrumbs in a basin and add the butter cut into small pieces. Warm the milk and pour it over the crumbs. Leave to stand for 10 minutes, then beat in the cheese.

3. Separate the eggs and beat the yolks into the crumb mixture. Season well with salt and pepper. Whisk the egg whites stiffly and fold in.

4. Pour the mixture over the tomatoes and sprinkle with the Cheesy Crumb Topping.

5. Bake at 400°F/200°C (Gas Mark 6) for 25-30 minutes or until golden and lightly set.

CAULIFLOWER BAKE

Imperial (Metric)	American
1 large cauliflower	1 large cauliflower
2 oz (50g) mushrooms	1 cupful mushrooms
3 oz (75g) polyunsaturated margarine	½ cupful polyunsaturated margarine
1 medium onion	1 medium onion
4 oz (100g) rolled oats	1 cupful rolled oats
2 eggs, separated	2 eggs, separated
Seasoning	Seasoning
Cheesy Crumb Topping (Page 17)	Cheesy Crumb Topping (Page 17)

1. Wash the cauliflower and divide into florets. Cook in boiling salted water until barely tender. Do not over-cook. Drain well and reserve.

2. Chop the mushrooms and onion. Melt 2 oz (50g) margarine in a large frying pan (skillet) and cook the mushrooms, onions and oats for about 15 minutes over moderate heat, stirring occasionally. Remove from the heat.

3. Cream the remaining margarine and beat in the egg yolks. Add to the oat mixture. Mix well and stir in the cauliflower. Whisk the egg whites stiffly and fold them in.

4. Transfer the mixture to a greased ovenproof dish, top with the Cheesy Crumb Topping and bake at 375°F/190°C (Gas Mark 5) for 30-35 minutes.

CAULIFLOWER, CELERY AND WALNUT BAKE

Imperial (Metric)	American
1 medium cauliflower	1 medium cauliflower
2 sticks celery	2 stalks celery
2 oz (50g) walnuts, chopped	½ cupful chopped English walnuts
3 oz (75g) soft wholemeal breadcrumbs	1½ cupsful soft wholewheat breadcrumbs
¼ pint (150ml) milk	⅔ cupful milk
4 eggs	4 eggs
2 oz (50g) butter	¼ cupful butter
2 oz (50g) grated cheese	½ cupful grated cheese
Seasoning to taste	Seasoning to taste
Cheesy Crumb Topping (Page 17)	Cheesy Crumb Topping (Page 17)

1. Trim the cauliflower and break into florets. Cook in boiling salted water until barely tender. Drain. Chop the celery and cook quickly in a little water until just tender. Drain. Mix with the chopped walnuts.

2. While the vegetables are cooking, soak the breadcrumbs in the milk. Melt the butter in a small pan and separate the eggs. Beat the egg yolks into the soaked breadcrumbs with the melted butter. Add the grated cheese and season well with salt and pepper.

3. Place the cauliflower, celery and walnuts in a pie dish or deep ovenproof dish. Beat the egg whites until stiff, fold into the bread mixture and pour over the cauliflower. Sprinkle with topping.

4. Stand the dish in a baking tin of hot water and bake at 350°F/180°C (Gas Mark 4) for about 30 minutes or until just firm.

EGG AND CELERY PIE

Imperial (Metric)	American
4 oz (100g) long grain brown rice	½ cupful long grain brown rice
4 eggs	4 eggs
2 sticks celery	2 stalks celery
2 oz (50g) blanched almonds	½ cupful blanched almonds
½ pint (¼ litre) White Sauce (page 23)	1⅓ cupsful White Sauce (page 23)
Lemon juice	Lemon juice
Seasoning to taste	Seasoning to taste
3 tablespoonsful fresh wholemeal breadcrumbs	3 tablespoonsful fresh wholewheat breadcrumbs
½ oz (15g) butter	1½ tablespoonsful butter
1 tablespoonful chopped parsley	1 tablespoonful chopped parsley

1. Cook the rice in plenty of boiling salted water and drain well.

2. Hard-boil the eggs, cool and slice. Chop the celery and almonds and mix together.

3. Make the white sauce and add a good squeeze of lemon juice.

4. Grease an ovenproof dish and make layers of rice, eggs, celery mixture and white sauce, seasoning lightly between the layers. Top with the breadcrumbs and dot with butter.

5. Bake at 375°F/190°C (Gas Mark 5) for about 25 minutes, or until hot through and browned. Garnish with chopped parsley.

STEWS, HOT POTS AND BAKES

PAPRIKA VEGETABLE HOT POT

Imperial (Metric)
6 oz (150g) dried red kidney beans, soaked
1 large onion
Vegetable oil
1 teaspoonful light soft raw cane sugar
3 medium carrots
½ lb (¼ kilo) white turnip
4 oz (100g) cooked chestnuts
1 red or green pepper
2 oz (50g) barley kernels
12 dried prunes, stoned
1 tablespoonful paprika or to taste
2 teaspoonsful dried thyme or marjoram
2 bay leaves
Seasoning to taste
1 pint (½ litre) dry white wine
Lemon juice to taste
1 lb (½ kilo) potatoes
Butter
Ground nutmeg

American
1 cupful dried red kidney beans, soaked
1 large onion
Vegetable oil
1 teaspoonful light soft raw cane sugar
3 medium carrots
8 ounces white turnip
4 ounces cooked chestnuts
1 red or green pepper
¼ cupful barley kernels
12 dried prunes, stoned
1 tablespoonful paprika or to taste
2 teaspoonsful dried thyme or marjoram
2 bay leaves
Seasoning to taste
2½ cupsful dry white wine
Lemon juice to taste
1 pound potatoes
Butter
Ground nutmeg

1. Drain and rinse the beans and cook in fresh water to cover until just soft. Drain.

2. Peel and chop the onion and fry in a little oil until beginning to brown. Sprinkle with the sugar and fry for a further 2-3 minutes.

3. Scrape the carrots and cut into thin rounds or strips. Peel and dice the turnip. Fry briskly with the onion, stirring well, for 3-4 minutes.

4. Transfer to a fireproof casserole, add the chestnuts, the pepper cut into thin strips, the barley kernels and prunes. Add paprika, herbs and seasoning and the cooked beans and pour in the wine. Cover and bring to the boil, then cook in the oven at 350°F/180°C (Gas Mark 4) for about 40 minutes or until the vegetables are tender.

5. While the vegetables are cooking, peel the potatoes and cut into thin rounds. Blanch in boiling salted water for 4-5 minutes or until almost cooked. Drain.

6. Remove the casserole from the oven. If the liquid has reduced too much add a little water, but do not cover the vegetables completely. Adjust the seasoning and add lemon juice to taste.

7. Cover with overlapping rounds of potato, dot with butter and season lightly with salt, pepper and nutmeg. Raise oven heat to 375°F/190°C (Gas Mark 5) and replace the casserole, uncovered, for about 20 minutes or until the potatoes are cooked through and browned. It may be further browned under the grill if you wish.

PROVENÇAL VEGETABLE STEW

Imperial (Metric)	American
4 oz (100g) dried red kidney beans	⅔ cupful dried red kidney beans
4 cloves garlic	4 cloves garlic
3 large onions	3 large onions
Vegetable oil	Vegetable oil
1 large carrot	1 large carrot
1 small green pepper	1 small green pepper
1 small red pepper	1 small red pepper
14 oz (400g) tin tomatoes	1 medium can tomatoes
12 stuffed olives	12 stuffed olives
2 teaspoonful fresh basil, chopped, or 1 teaspoonful dried basil	2 teaspoonful fresh basil, chopped, or 1 teaspoonful dried basil
2 teaspoonful fresh marjoram, chopped, or 1 teaspoonful dried marjoram	2 teaspoonful fresh marjoram, chopped, or 1 teaspoonful dried marjoram
Seasoning to taste	Seasoning to taste
½ pint (¼ litre) red wine	1⅓ cupful red wine
3 teaspoonful arrowroot	3 teaspoonful arrowroot
Chopped parsley	Chopped parsley

1. Soak the beans either overnight or in very hot water for 1-2 hours. Drain.

2. Peel and chop the garlic and onions and fry them together in a little oil until beginning to brown. Transfer to a flameproof casserole with the drained beans.

3. Scrape and dice the carrot, de-seed and slice the peppers and add them to the casserole with the tomatoes and their juice, the stuffed olives, herbs and seasonings.

4. Pour in the red wine, bring to the boil and simmer for 10 minutes.

5. Transfer the casserole to the oven and cook, covered, at 325°F/170°C (Gas Mark 3) for about 1½ hours or until the beans are soft and vegetables tender.

6. Mix the arrowroot with a little water, stir into the casserole and simmer over medium heat for a few minutes until thickened. Serve sprinkled with chopped parsley.

CHICK PEA AND VEGETABLE CASSEROLE

Imperial (Metric)	American
½ lb (¼ kilo) chick peas	1 cupful garbanzo beans
1 aubergine, about ¾ lb (350g)	1 eggplant (about 12 ounces)
1 medium onion	1 medium onion
1 clove garlic	1 clove garlic
1 small leek	1 small leek
Vegetable oil	Vegetable oil
14 oz (400g) tin tomatoes	1 medium can tomatoes
¼ pint (150ml) vegetable stock (page 29)	⅔ cupful vegetable stock (page 29)
½ teaspoonful ground ginger	½ teaspoonful ground ginger
Pinch each ground cloves and nutmeg	Pinch each ground cloves and nutmeg
Seasoning to taste	Seasoning to taste
3 teaspoonsful arrowroot	3 teaspoonsful arrowroot
2 slices wholemeal bread	2 slices wholewheat bread
½ oz (15g) butter or polyunsaturated margarine	1½ tablespoonsful butter or polyunsaturated margarine

1. Soak the chick peas (garbanzo beans) in cold water overnight, or cover with boiling water and soak for 2-3 hours. Drain, cover with fresh cold water, bring to the boil and simmer for about 1-1½ hours until soft. Drain.

2. While the chick peas (garbanzo beans) are cooking, peel and slice the aubergine (eggplant) thickly, sprinkle with salt and leave it for 30 minutes. Rinse, drain and dry. Cut the aubergine (eggplant) into large dice.

3. Peel and chop the onion and garlic. Split the leek, wash it thoroughly, drain and cut it into short lengths. Fry onion, garlic, leek and aubergine (eggplant) briskly in a little oil for about 10 minutes.

4. Transfer the vegetables to a casserole and add the tomatoes and their juice, the stock, spices and seasoning. Stir in the chick peas (garbanzo beans).

5. Cover and bake at 350°F/180°C (Gas Mark 4) for about 30 minutes. Blend the arrowroot with a little water. Remove the casserole from the oven and stir in the arrowroot mixture.

6. Melt the butter or margarine, brush over the slices of bread. Cut the bread into triangles and arrange on top of the vegetables.

7. Raise the heat to 400°F/200°C (Gas Mark 6). Replace the casserole in the oven and cook uncovered for a further 15 minutes.

WINTER VEGETABLE CASSEROLE

Imperial (Metric)	American
2 large onions	2 large onions
2 cloves garlic	2 cloves garlic
2 sticks celery	2 stalks celery
2 carrots	2 carrots
4 oz (100g) parsnip, diced	2/3 cupful diced parsnip
4 oz (100g) swede, diced	2/3 cupful diced rutabaga
4 oz (100g) green pepper	1 medium green pepper
4 oz (100g) mushrooms	2 cupsful mushrooms
Vegetable oil	Vegetable oil
14 oz (400g) tin tomatoes	1 medium can tomatoes
1 pint (1/2 litre) vegetable stock (page 29)	2 1/2 cupsful vegetable stock (page 29)
1 teaspoonful dried thyme	1 teaspoonful dried thyme
1 tablespoonful chopped parsley	1 tablespoonful chopped parsley
1 bay leaf	1 bay leaf
Dash of Tabasco sauce	Dash of Tabasco sauce
Seasoning to taste	Seasoning to taste
2 teaspoonsful arrowroot	2 teaspoonsful arrowroot
Dumplings (page 20)	Dumplings (page 20)

1. Peel and chop the onions and garlic. Scrub and chop the celery and carrots. Remove seeds and chop the pepper. Wipe the mushrooms and slice if large.

2. Fry the onions and garlic gently in vegetable oil until beginning to brown. Add the other chopped vegetables and fry together for 5-6 minutes, stirring well.

3. Add the tomatoes and their juice, the stock, herbs and Tabasco. Season with salt and pepper. Transfer to a casserole, cover and cook in the oven at 325°F/170°C (Gas Mark 3) for about 1 hour, or until the vegetables are tender. Check the seasoning.

4. Make the dumplings. Remove the casserole from the oven and raise oven heat to 400°F/200°C (Gas Mark 6).

5. Blend the arrowroot with a little water and stir it into the casserole. Place the dumplings on top, replace the lid and bake for a further 15 minutes.

COURGETTE AND TOMATO COBBLER

Imperial (Metric)
1 medium onion
2 cloves garlic
Vegetable oil
4 tomatoes, or equivalent in tinned
  tomatoes
1½ lb (¾ kilo) courgettes
1 teaspoonful coriander seeds
2 teaspoonsful chopped fresh basil
  or 1 teaspoonful dried basil
Seasoning to taste
Cobbler Topping (page 19)

American
1 medium onion
2 cloves garlic
Vegetable oil
4 tomatoes, or equivalent in canned
  tomatoes
1½ pounds zucchini
1 teaspoonful coriander seeds
2 teaspoonsful chopped fresh basil
  or 1 teaspoonful dried basil
Seasoning to taste
Cobbler Topping (page 19)

1. Peel and chop the onion and garlic and fry them gently in a little oil until beginning to soften.

2. Skin and chop the tomatoes. Wash the courgettes (zucchini), trim and cut into thick slices. Mix them with the onions and transfer the mixture to a casserole. Crush the coriander and stir it into the vegetables with the basil and salt and pepper to taste.

3. Cover and bake at 325°F/170°C (Gas Mark 3) for about 45 minutes or until the courgettes (zucchini) are beginning to soften. Remove the casserole from the oven and turn the heat up to 400°F/200°C (Gas Mark 6).

4. Arrange rounds of topping over the vegetables and return the casserole to the oven for 20 minutes, or until the topping is brown and well risen.

BEAN AND VEGETABLE COBBLER

Imperial (Metric)	American
½ lb (¼ kilo) onions	½ pound onions
1 small leek	1 small leek
2 cloves garlic	2 cloves garlic
1 lb (½ kilo) mixed root vegetables	1 pound mixed root vegetables
2 oz (50g) butter or polyunsaturated margarine	¼ cupful butter or polyunsaturated margarine
Seasoning to taste	Seasoning to taste
4 tablespoonsful chopped parsley	4 tablespoonsful chopped parsley
4 oz (100g) cooked beans, any kind	⅔ cupful cooked beans, any kind
¼ pint (150ml) White Sauce (page 23)	⅔ cupful White Sauce (page 23)
Cobbler Topping (page 19)	Cobbler Topping (page 19)

1. Peel and chop the onions. Trim the leek, wash it thoroughly and cut it into short lengths. Simmer the onion and leek in lightly salted water to cover until beginning to soften. Drain them well, reserving the cooking water.

2. Peel and chop the garlic. Peel or scrape the root vegetables and cut them into small dice. Melt the butter in a frying pan and fry the onion, garlic and root vegetables over a moderate heat for 10 minutes, stirring well with a wooden spoon. Cover and continue cooking gently for 10 minutes.

3. Season the vegetables well, mix in the cooked beans and parsley and transfer the mixture to a pie dish.

4. Make the white sauce, using half milk and half reserved cooking water from the onions and leeks. Spoon it over the vegetables in the pie dish.

5. Cover with the rounds of Cobbler Topping and bake at 400°F/200°C (Gas Mark 6) for 20 minutes.

NOODLES BAKED WITH CREAM SAUCE

Imperial (Metric)	American
¾ lb (350g) wholemeal noodles	1½ cupsful wholewheat noodles
1 large onion	1 large onion
1 clove garlic	1 clove garlic
½ lb (¼ kilo) cottage cheese	1 cupful cottage cheese
¼ pint (150ml) soured cream	⅔ cupful soured cream
1 tablespoonful *Holbrook's* Worcester sauce	1 tablespoonful *Holbrook's* Worcester sauce
Cayenne pepper	Cayenne pepper
Butter	Butter
Grated cheese	Grated cheese

1. Cook the noodles in boiling salted water until just tender. Drain, rinse under running cold water and drain again thoroughly.

2. While the noodles are cooking, peel the onion and garlic and chop finely.

3. Mix the onion and garlic with the cottage cheese and soured cream, stir in the noodles and season with Worcester sauce and a good pinch of cayenne.

4. Butter an ovenproof dish, spoon in the noodle mixture and bake at 400°F/200°C (Gas Mark 6) for about 30 minutes or until hot through and lightly browned. Serve with grated cheese.

CHEESE AND SPAGHETTI BAKE

Imperial (Metric)	American
½ lb (¼ kilo) wholemeal spaghetti	8 ounces wholewheat spaghetti
¾ lb (350g) mushrooms, sliced	4½ cupsful sliced mushrooms
4 oz (100g) butter	½ cupful butter
3 tomatoes, skinned and chopped	3 tomatoes, skinned and chopped
6 oz (150g) Cheddar cheese, coarsley grated	1½ cupsful coarsely grated Cheddar cheese
6 oz (150g) tofu, drained and cubed	1 cupful tofu, drained and cubed
Seasoning to taste	Seasoning to taste

1. Cooking the spaghetti in boiling salted water until barely tender. Drain it well, rinse it under cold water and drain again.

2. Fry the mushrooms gently in half the butter until they are soft and the juices begin to run. Mix them well with the spaghetti, chopped tomatoes and cubes of tofu.

3. Place half the cheese in the bottom of a deep ovenproof dish, cover with the spaghetti mixture and top with the remaining cheese.

4. Bake at 375°F/190°C (Gas Mark 5) for about 30 minutes, or until the cheese is bubbly and lightly browned.

SPAGHETTI BAKE WITH NUTS AND OLIVES

Imperial (Metric)	American
6 oz (150g) wholemeal spaghetti	6 ounces wholewheat spaghetti
¾ pint (400ml) White Sauce (see page 23 for method)	2 cupsful White Sauce (see page 23 for method)
Seasoning to taste	Seasoning to taste
1 teaspoonful dry mustard	1 teaspoonful dry mustard
½ teaspoonful paprika	½ teaspoonful paprika
1 tablespoonful grated onion	1 tablespoonful grated onion
½ oz (15g) polyunsaturated margarine	1½ tablespoonsful polyunsaturated margarine
18 stuffed olives, chopped	18 stuffed olives, chopped
4 oz (100g) mixed nuts, finely chopped	1 cupful chopped mixed nuts
4 oz (100g) grated cheese	1 cupful grated cheese
Cheesy Crumb Topping (Page 17)	Cheesy Crumb Topping (Page 17)
3-4 tomatoes, sliced	3-4 tomatoes, sliced

1. Break the spaghetti into short lengths and cook in boiling salted water until just tender. Drain well.

2. While the spaghetti is cooking make the white sauce. This should be well thickened but not stiff. Season the sauce with salt and pepper, mustard, paprika and grated onion.

3. Mix the sauce with the cooked spaghetti.

4. Grease a casserole with the margarine and make layers of spaghetti, sprinkling each layer with olives, nuts and cheese.

5. Sprinkle with the topping and arrange the tomato slices in a border.

6. Bake at 350°F/180°C (Gas Mark 4) for about 30 minutes.

CHEESE AND SWEETCORN BAKE

Imperial (Metric)
½ green pepper
1 oz (25g) butter or polyunsaturated
  margarine
1 oz (25g) 81% wholemeal flour
½ pint (250ml) milk
4 oz (100g) grated cheese
3 eggs, separated
4 oz (100g) cooked sweetcorn
  kernels, fresh, frozen or canned
1 teaspoonful sea salt
1 teaspoonful paprika

American
½ green pepper
2½ tablespoonsful butter or
  polyunsaturated margarine
¼ cupful 81% wholemeal flour
1⅓ cupsful milk
1 cupful grated cheese
3 eggs, separated
1 cupful cooked sweetcorn kernels,
  fresh, frozen or canned
1 teaspoonful sea salt
1 teaspoonful paprika

1. De-seed and chop the green pepper and fry gently in the butter or margarine until just tender.

2. Blend in the flour and add the milk slowly, stirring well. Cook until thick. Add the grated cheese and stir over low heat until the cheese has melted. Turn mixture into a bowl and cool slightly.

3. Beat the egg yolks and add to the cheese mixture with the corn, salt and paprika. Leave to continue cooling for 10 minutes.

4. Whisk the egg whites until stiff. Mix about half with the corn mixture and fold the remainder in lightly.

5. Grease a casserole and spoon in the mixture. Bake at 350°F/180°C (Gas Mark 4) for about 45 minutes or until well risen and just set.

ALMOND TOPPED VEGETABLE PIE

Imperial (Metric)	American
1½ lb (750g) leeks	1½ pounds leeks
½ lb (250g) mushrooms	4 cupsful mushrooms
1 oz (25g) butter or polyunsaturated margarine	2½ tablespoonsful butter or polyunsaturated margarine
White sauce made with ½ pint (250ml) mixed milk and cooking water from leeks (see page 23 for method)	White sauce made with 1⅓ cupsful mixed milk and cooking water from leeks (see page 23 for method)
1 lb (500g) potatoes, cooked, cooled slightly and mashed	1 pound potatoes, cooked, cooled slightly and mashed
4 tablespoonsful mayonnaise	4 tablespoonsful mayonnaise
Seasoning to taste	Seasoning to taste
1 tablespoonful chopped chives or spring onions	1 tablespoonful chopped chives or scallions
2 tablespoonsful beaten egg	2 tablespoonsful beaten egg
2 oz (50g) almonds, blanched, chopped and lightly toasted	½ cupful almonds, blanched, chopped and lightly toasted

1. Wash the leeks thoroughly, cut into short lengths and cook in salted water to cover until barely tender. Drain well, reserving the cooking water.

2. Slice the mushrooms and fry gently in butter or margarine until soft.

3. Make the white sauce, using a mixture of half milk and half cooking water from the leeks.

4. Mix the leeks, mushrooms and white sauce and spoon into a pie dish.

5. Mix the mashed potato with the mayonnaise and chopped chives or spring onions. Season well. Spread over the leek and mushroom mixture.

6. Brush the potato with beaten egg. Sprinkle the toasted almonds on top and bake at 350°F/180°C (Gas Mark 4) for about 30 minutes or until hot through and lightly browned.

AUBERGINE AND ONION BAKE

Imperial (Metric)	American
1½ lb (750g) aubergine	1½ pounds eggplant
2 large onions	2 large onions
2 cloves garlic	2 cloves garlic
Vegetable oil	Vegetable oil
4 medium eggs	4 medium eggs
2 oz (50g) 81% wholemeal flour	½ cupful 81% wholewheat flour
1 tablespoonful chopped parsley	1 tablespoonful chopped parsley
½ teaspoonful chopped thyme	½ teaspoonful chopped thyme
Seasoning to taste	Seasoning to taste

1. Cut the aubergine (eggplant) into thick slices, sprinkle well with salt and leave for 30 minutes. Wash slices well, drain and dry on paper towels.

2. Fry the aubergine (eggplant) slices in a little vegetable oil over medium heat, turning once, until soft. Drain well and reserve.

3. Peel and chop the onion and garlic and fry in the same oil until soft and beginning to brown.

4. Scoop the flesh from the aubergine (eggplant) slices with a knife or teaspoon and discard the skins. Mix the pulp with the cooked onion.

5. Beat in the eggs, flour, herbs and seasoning. Spread out in a shallow baking tin so that the mixture is about 1 inch (2.5cm) deep.

6. Bake at 400°F/200°C (Gas Mark 6) for about 20-30 minutes or until just firm and lightly browned. Cut into slices and serve hot or cold.

Note: Serves 6-8 as a first course with mixed salad.

MUSHROOM-NUT BAKE

Imperial (Metric)	American
4 oz (100g) fresh wholemeal breadcrumbs	2 cupsful fresh wholewheat breadcrumbs
2 oz (50g) ground almonds	1/2 cupful ground almonds
1-2 cloves garlic	1-2 cloves garlic
3 oz (75g) butter or polyunsaturated margarine	7 1/2 tablespoonsful butter or polyunsaturated margarine
1 teaspoonful dried mixed herbs	1 teaspoonful dried mixed herbs
2 teaspoonsful chopped parsley	2 teaspoonsful chopped parsley
4 oz (100g) chopped or flaked almonds	3/4 cupful chopped or slivered almonds
3/4 lb (350g) mushrooms	6 cupsful mushrooms
1/2 pint (1/4 litre) White Sauce (page 23)	1 1/3 cupsful White Sauce (page 23)
Ground nutmeg	Ground nutmeg
Seasoning to taste	Seasoning to taste
2 tomatoes	2 tomatoes
Vegetable oil	Vegetable oil

1. Mix the breadcrumbs and the ground almonds in a bowl. Crush the garlic and add it to the mixture. Rub in 2 oz (50g)/5 tablespoonsful butter or polyunsaturated margarine. Stir in the herbs and the flaked (slivered) almonds.

2. Turn the mixture into a lightly greased ovenproof dish, press it down firmly and bake at 425°F/220°C (Gas Mark 7) for 10-15 minutes or until lightly browned and crisp.

3. Wash the mushrooms and dry them on paper towelling. Set 3 or 4 aside for garnish and slice the rest.

4. Heat the remaining butter or margarine in a pan and fry the sliced mushrooms briskly. Mix with the white sauce and season with nutmeg and salt and pepper.

5. Spoon the mixture over the nut base and spread it evenly. Slice the tomatoes and then arrange on top with the remaining mushrooms.

6. Brush with oil and season lightly. Return to the oven for 10-15
    minutes.

APPLE AND PARSNIP BAKE

Imperial (Metric)	American
1 lb (½ kilo) parsnips	1 pound parsnips
1 oz (25g) polyunsaturated margarine	2½ tablespoonsful polyunsaturated margarine
Seasoning to taste	Seasoning to taste
¾ lb (350g) cooking apples	12 ounces cooking apples
1 tablespoonful soft raw cane sugar	1 tablespoonful soft raw cane sugar
Juice of ½ lemon	Juice of ½ lemon
½ teaspoonful grated nutmeg	½ teaspoonful grated nutmeg

1. Peel and chop the parsnips and cook them in boiling salted water until just tender. Drain well and mash them with the margarine. Season to taste with salt and pepper.

2. Spoon half the mashed parsnip into an ovenproof dish.

3. Peel, core and slice the apples and arrange them over the parsnip *purée*. Top with the remaining parsnip.

4. Sprinkle with brown sugar, lemon juice and nutmeg.

5. Cover and bake at 350°F/180°C (Gas Mark 4) for 20-30 minutes.

6. Remove the lid and place the dish under the grill for a few minutes to brown. A further sprinkling of sugar may be added at this stage if you wish.

POTATO BAKE WITH TOFU

Imperial (Metric)	American
4 large baking potatoes	4 large baking potatoes
2 oz (50g) butter or polyunsaturated margarine	5 tablespoonsful butter or polyunsaturated margarine
Seasoning to taste	Seasoning to taste
4 oz (100g) grated cheese	1 cupful grated cheese
½ teaspoonful dry mustard	½ teaspoonful dry mustard
¼ pint (150ml) thin cream	⅔ cupful light cream
3 tablespoonsful chopped parsley	3 tablespoonsful chopped parsley
6 oz (150g) tofu	1 cupful tofu
Vegetable oil	Vegetable oil

1. Peel the potatoes and cut into chips. Take a large piece of kitchen foil and spread it out on a baking tray. There should be enough overlap to make a large parcel.

2. Place the potatoes on the foil and dot with butter. Season well with salt and pepper.

3. Mix the grated cheese with the mustard and sprinkle it over the potatoes with the cream and half the chopped parsley.

4. Fold the edges of the foil together to seal but do not press down on the potatoes.

5. Bake at 450°F/230°C (Gas Mark 8) for 45-50 minutes.

6. Drain the tofu, cut it into slices and fry it in shallow oil until brown, turning once to brown second side.

7. Place the foil parcel on a serving dish and open it carefully, folding the foil back to the edges. Top the potatoes with the tofu slices and sprinkle with the rest of the parsley.

CELERY AND WALNUT BAKE

Imperial (Metric)	American
1 large head celery	1 large head celery
2 oz (50g) walnuts, chopped	½ cupful chopped English walnuts
6 slices wholemeal bread	6 slices wholewheat bread
½ oz (15g) butter or polyunsaturated margarine	1½ tablespoonsful butter or polyunsaturated margarine
4 oz (100g) cheese, grated	1 cupful grated cheese
3 eggs	3 eggs
¾ pint (400ml) milk	2 cupsful milk
1 medium onion	1 medium onion
Seasoning	Seasoning
Pinch dry mustard	Pinch dry mustard

1. Trim the celery, reserving some leaves for garnish. Cut the celery into short lengths and wash well. Cook it in boiling salted water for about 10 minutes or until just tender. Drain well.

2. Trim the crusts from the bread (crusts may be made into breadcrumbs for another use). Cut large rounds from the slices with a pastry cutter and set aside. Break up the bread trimmings into small pieces.

3. Grease a casserole with the butter or margarine and place the bread trimmings in the bottom. Sprinkle the cheese over the bread and top with the celery and walnuts.

4. Arrange the bread rounds on top of the casserole. Beat the eggs and mix with the milk. Grate in the onion and season with salt, pepper and mustard powder. Pour the mix over the casserole, cover and refrigerate for 1 hour.

5. Bake, uncovered, at 350°F/180°C (Gas Mark 4), for about 1 hour 15 minutes. The custard should be set and the top well browned. Garnish with the celery leaves.

SAVOURY YORKSHIRE PUDDING

Imperial (Metric)
4 oz (100g) plain 81% wholemeal flour
1/4 teaspoonful salt
1 egg plus 1 yolk
1/2 pint (1/4 litre) milk and water, mixed
Dash *Holbrook's* Worcester sauce
1/4 teaspoonful caraway seeds
Pinch dried tarragon
Pinch dried basil
4 small onions
6 tomatoes or equivalent in tinned tomatoes
2-3 oz (50-75g) mushrooms
Vegetable oil

American
1 cupful plain 81% wholewheat flour
1/4 teaspoonful salt
1 egg plus 1 yolk
1 1/3 cupsful milk and water, mixed
Dash *Holbrook's* Worcester sauce
1/4 teaspoonful caraway seeds
Pinch dried tarragon
Pinch dried basil
4 small onions
6 tomatoes or equivalent in canned tomatoes
1-1 1/2 cupsful mushrooms
Vegetable oil

1. Mix the flour and salt. Use with the egg, egg yolk and milk to make a batter (for method, see Pancakes, page 22). Stir in the Worcester sauce and herbs. Leave to stand in a cool place while preparing the vegetables.

2. Peel the onions and cook in boiling salted water until tender. Drain well.

3. Skin the tomatoes or, if using tinned tomatoes, drain well.

4. Slice the mushrooms and fry briskly in a little oil until soft.

5. Set the oven to 425°F/220°C (Gas Mark 7). Heat 2-3 tablespoonsful oil in a rectangular baking tin until hot. Spoon the vegetables into the hot oil, taking care as the oil may sputter. Replace in the oven until the oil is once more very hot.

6. Pour the batter carefully into the tin, replace in the oven and cook for 20-25 minutes or until the batter is set and well risen.

POTATO-TOP PIE

Imperial (Metric)	American
1¼ lb (600g) potatoes	1¼ pounds potatoes
4 eggs	4 eggs
4 oz (100g) mushrooms	2 cupsful mushrooms
4 oz (100g) fresh or frozen peas	⅔ cupful fresh or frozen peas
Butter or polyunsaturated margarine	Butter or polyunsaturated margarine
1 tablespoonful chopped parsley	1 tablespoonful chopped parsley
Seasoning to taste	Seasoning to taste
1 teaspoonful chopped lovage (optional)	1 teaspoonful chopped lovage (optional)
¼ pint (150ml) vegetable stock (page 29)	⅔ cupful vegetable stock (page 29)
4 oz (100g) grated cheese	1 cupful grated cheese

1. Cook the potatoes in boiling salted water until just tender. Drain and slice them. Hard-boil the eggs, shell and slice them. Slice the mushrooms. Cook the peas and drain.

2. Grease a pie dish with butter or margarine. Make layers of the vegetables and sliced eggs, finishing with potatoes, sprinkling with herbs and seasoning between the layers.

3. Pour the stock over the vegetables, sprinkle with the cheese and bake at 350°F/180°C (Gas Mark 4) for 30-40 minutes.

POTATO AND MUSHROOM BAKE

Imperial (Metric)	American
1 lb (½ kilo) potatoes	1 pound potatoes
½ lb (¼ kilo) mushrooms	4 cupsful mushrooms
1 clove garlic	1 clove garlic
2 oz (50g) butter	¼ cupful butter
2 tablespoonsful finely chopped onion	2 tablespoonsful finely chopped onion
2-3 tablespoonsful chopped parsley	2-3 tablespoonsful chopped parsley
Seasoning to taste	Seasoning to taste
½ pint (¼ litre) milk or single cream	1⅓ cupsful milk or light cream
3-4 tablespoonsful grated cheese	3-4 tablespoonsful grated cheese

1. Peel the potatoes and slice them very thinly. Slice the mushrooms.

2. Rub an ovenproof dish well with the cut garlic clove and then with a little butter.

3. Arrange the potatoes and mushrooms in the dish in layers, sprinkling as you go with chopped onion and parsley and seasoning with salt and pepper. Dot each layer with butter.

4. Pour the milk over the dish and sprinkle with the cheese.

5. Cover with foil and bake at 325°F/170°C (Gas Mark 3) for about 1½ hours, or until potatoes are soft and creamy, removing the foil for the last 30 minutes of cooking.

MOUSSAKA

Imperial (Metric)	American
½ lb (¼ kilo) aubergine	8 ounces eggplant
½ lb (¼ kilo) celeriac	8 ounces celeriac
½ lb (¼ kilo) potatoes	8 ounces potatoes
Vegetable oil	Vegetable oil
Tomato Sauce (page 27)	Tomato Sauce (page 27)
¾ pint (400ml) Cheese Sauce (page 24)	2 cupsful Cheese Sauce (page 24)
Yolk of 1 egg	Yolk of 1 egg

1. Wash and dry the aubergine (eggplant). Cut it into fairly thick slices, unpeeled, and sprinkle well with salt. Leave it for 30 minutes.

2. Meanwhile, peel the celeriac and shred or grate it coarsely. Blanch it for 1 minute in boiling salted water and drain well.

3. Peel the potatoes and cut them into slices about ¼ in. (6mm) thick. Fry them in deep or shallow oil until they are brown on both sides and beginning to soften. Drain well.

4. Rinse the aubergine (eggplant) slices, drain and pat them dry on kitchen paper. Fry them in oil, turning once, until well browned. Drain.

5. Place half the potato slices in a large ovenproof dish and spread them with tomato sauce. Add the drained celeriac, topped with a few spoonsful of cheese sauce.

6. Follow with the aubergine (eggplant), the remaining tomato sauce and finally the remaining potatoes.

7. Beat the egg yolk into the rest of the cheese sauce and spread it over the potatoes.

8. Bake at 350°F/180°C (Gas Mark 4) for about 30 minutes, or until hot and bubbling.

COURGETTE AND PEPPER CASSEROLE

Imperial (Metric)	American
1 lb (½ kilo) courgettes	1 pound zucchini
1 oz (25g) butter	2½ tablespoonsful butter
Seasoning to taste	Seasoning to taste
1 green pepper	1 green pepper
1 medium onion	1 medium onion
Vegetable oil	Vegetable oil
Tabasco sauce (optional)	Tabasco sauce (optional)
4 eggs	4 eggs
4 tablespoonsful thin cream or top of milk	4 tablespoonsful thin cream or top of milk
3-4 tablespoonsful grated cheese	3-4 tablespoonsful grated cheese

1. Trim the courgettes (zucchini) and slice them thinly. Cook them in boiling salted water for 2-3 minutes or until barely tender. Drain well.

2. Melt the butter and mix it with the drained courgettes. Spoon them into a baking dish and season with salt and pepper.

3. Remove all seeds and membranes and chop the pepper. Peel and chop the onion. Fry the pepper and onion briskly in a little oil until soft. Season them with salt and pepper and a dash of Tabasco if you wish, and spoon them over the courgettes (zucchini).

4. Beat the eggs with the cream and season with salt and pepper. Pour the mixture over the vegetables and sprinkle with cheese.

5. Bake at 450°F/230°C (Gas Mark 8) for about 15 minutes or until the egg mixture is set.

GNOCCHI WITH TOMATO SAUCE

Imperial (Metric)	American
1 pint (½ litre) milk	2½ cupsful milk
1 onion, peeled and halved	1 onion, peeled and halved
1 bay leaf	1 bay leaf
5 oz (125g) cornmeal (polenta)	1¼ cupsful cornmeal (polenta)
Seasoning to taste	Seasoning to taste
4 oz (100g) grated cheese	1 cupful grated cheese
½ oz (15g) butter or polyunsaturated margarine	1½ tablespoonsful butter or polyunsaturated margarine
1 teaspoonful made mustard	1 teaspoonful made mustard
Tomato Sauce (page 27)	Tomato Sauce (page 27)

1. Bring the milk to the boil with the onion and bay leaf. Turn off the heat and leave it to stand for 15 minutes.

2. Remove the onion and bay leaf, bring the milk back to the boil. Slowly stir in the cornmeal, off the heat. Season with salt and pepper.

3. Bring the mixture back to the boil and simmer for about 20 minutes, stirring well, until it is thick. Remove it from the heat and stir in 2 oz (50g) grated cheese, butter and mustard.

4. Spread the mixture out on a dish in a layer about ¾ in. (2cm) thick. When it is firm and quite cold, cut it into circles with a 1½ in. (4cm) cutter, or into small squares with a sharp knife.

5. Arrange the *gnocchi* in a shallow, greased ovenproof dish, sprinkle with the remaining cheese and bake at 400°F/200°C (Gas Mark 6) for 25 minutes or until hot through and browned. Serve with the tomato sauce.

SAVOURY BANANA BAKE

Imperial (Metric)	American
2 lb (1 kilo) green bananas	1 pounds green bananas
1 large onion	1 large onion
½ pint (¼ kilo) White Sauce (page 23)	1⅓ cupsful White Sauce (page 23)
Seasoning	Seasoning
½ teaspoonful paprika	½ teaspoonful paprika
Pinch curry powder	Pinch curry powder
4 oz (100g) grated cheese	1 cupful grated cheese

1. Peel the bananas (cut them in half and slit the skins lengthwise at intervals to make peeling easier). Slice the bananas and cook them in boiling salted water for 10 minutes. Drain them well. Slice the onion thinly.

2. Make a white sauce and season it with salt, pepper and paprika. Stir in half the cheese.

3. Make layers of bananas and onion in an ovenproof dish. Pour the sauce over and sprinkle with remaining cheese.

4. Bake at 375°F/190°C (Gas Mark 5) for about 1 hour, or until bananas are completely cooked.

POTATO AND YOGURT BAKE

Imperial (Metric)	American
1½ lb (¾ kilo) baking potatoes	1½ pounds potatoes
1 tablespoonful wine or cider vinegar	1 tablespoonful wine or cider vinegar
½ pint (¼ litre) natural yogurt	⅔ cupful natural yogurt
1 egg, beaten	1 egg, beaten
Seasoning	Seasoning
¼ teaspoonful grated nutmeg	¼ teaspoonful grated nutmeg
1 small onion, grated	1 small onion, grated
2 oz (50g) grated cheese	½ cupful grated cheese

1. Peel the potatoes and grate them coarsely. Place them in a bowl of salted water with the vinegar for 5 minutes. Drain them and press out as much moisture as possible.

2. Mix the potato with the yogurt, beaten egg, seasoning, nutmeg and onion.

3. Turn the mixture into a shallow ovenproof dish, sprinkle with the cheese and bake at 375°F/190°C (Gas Mark 5) for 40 minutes.

TOMATO AND MUSHROOM PANCAKE BAKE

Imperial (Metric)
4 oz (100g) mushrooms
Vegetable oil
White Sauce made with ½ pint (¼ litre) milk (page 23)
Seasoning to taste
4 oz (100g) cooked beans (any type)
Tomato Sauce (page 27)
12 × 6in. (15cm) Pancakes (page 22)
Soya Crumble Topping (page 18)
3-4 tablespoonsful grated Parmesan cheese

American
2 cupsful mushrooms
Vegetable oil
White Sauce made with 1⅓ cupsful milk (page 23)
Seasoning to taste
⅔ cupful cooked beans (any type)
Tomato Sauce (page 27)
12 × 6in. Crepes (page 22)
Soya Crumble Topping (page 18)
3-4 tablespoonsful grated Parmesan cheese

1. Wash, dry and slice the mushrooms and fry them quickly in a little oil until beginning to soften. Drain.

2. Mix the mushrooms with the white sauce and adjust seasoning. Mix the cooked beans with the tomato sauce.

3. Layer the pancakes in an ovenproof dish, overlapping two pancakes for each layer and spreading alternate layers with mushroom mixture and with bean and tomato mixture. Finish with white sauce and mushrooms.

4. Sprinkle with the Soya Crumble Mix and bake at 375°F/190°C (Gas Mark 5) for 25-30 minutes. Sprinkle with the Parmesan cheese before serving.

COCONUT LAYER

Imperial (Metric)	American
¾ lb (350g) aubergine	12 ounces eggplant
½ lb (¼ kilo) onions	8 ounces onions
½ lb (¼ kilo) green or red pepper	8 ounces green or red pepper
½ lb (¼ kilo) courgettes or cucumber	8 ounces zucchini or cucumber
Vegetable oil	Vegetable oil
4 medium bananas	4 medium bananas
4 oz (100g) fresh coconut, grated or shredded	1¼ cupsful fresh coconut, grated or shredded
¼ pint (150ml) fresh coconut milk	⅔ cupful fresh coconut milk
Seasoning to taste	Seasoning to taste
Good pinch each of ground cinnamon, cloves, ginger and nutmeg	Good pinch each of ground cinnamon, cloves, ginger and nutmeg
12 × 6in. (15cm) Pancakes (page 22)	12 × 6in. Crepes (page 22)
½ pint (¼ litre) Cheese Sauce (page 24)	1⅓ cupsful Cheese Sauce (page 24)

1. Peel the aubergine (eggplant), cut it into slices and sprinkle with salt. Leave it for 30 minutes, then rinse, drain and chop.

2. Peel and chop the onion. De-seed and chop the pepper. Peel and chop the courgettes (zucchini) or cucumber.

3. Fry the onion gently in a little oil until beginning to soften, then add the aubergine (eggplant), peppers and courgettes (zucchini). Fry them together over low heat for about 10 minutes, stirring well, then cover and leave to cook gently until quite soft.

4. Peel the bananas, slice and fry them for 5 minutes in a little oil in a separate pan. Remove the bananas and drain them. Fry the coconut in the same pan, stirring well, for about 10 minutes or until beginning to soften. Add the bananas and coconut to the vegetable mixture, stir in the coconut milk, mix well and season to taste with salt, pepper and spices.

5. Layer the pancakes in a shallow ovenproof dish, overlapping two
    pancakes for each layer and spreading each with the vegetable
    mixture. Finish with a layer of pancakes and spread with the cheese
    sauce.

6. Cover the dish with foil and bake at 375°F/190°C (Gas Mark
    5) for about 30 minutes or until hot and bubbling, removing the
    foil for the last 10 minutes of cooking. Cut into wedges to serve.

4.

STUFFED VEGETABLE DISHES

STUFFED ONIONS

Imperial (Metric)
4 large onions
1 oz (25g) polyunsaturated
  margarine
2 oz (50g) mushrooms, chopped
4 tablespoonsful dry Country Stuffing
  Mix
Butter
2 teaspoonsful grated lemon peel
Seasoning to taste
½ pint (¼ litre) vegetable stock
  (page 29)
2-3 slices stale wholemeal bread
Tomato Sauce (page 27) or
  Spicy Tomato Sauce (page 28)

American
4 large onions
2½ tablespoonsful polyunsaturated
  margarine
1½ cupsful chopped mushrooms
4 tablespoonsful dry Country Stuffing
  Mix
Butter
2 teaspoonsful grated lemon peel
Seasoning to taste
1⅓ cupsful vegetable stock
  (page 29)
2-3 slices stale wholewheat bread
Tomato Sauce (page 27) or
  Spicy Tomato Sauce (page 28)

1. Peel the onions and hollow out the centres with a sharp knife, leaving a shell about ½ in. (1cm) thick. Simmer the hollowed out onions in lightly salted boiling water until they begin to soften. Do not over cook them. Drain well, reserving the cooking water.

2. While the shells are cooking, chop about half the onion removed from the centres and fry it gently in the margarine with the mushrooms until soft.

3. Mix the dry stuffing mix with about 8 tablespoonsful of the water

used to cook the onions. Beat in a knob of butter.

4. Mix it with the cooked onion and mushrooms, add the grated lemon peel and salt and pepper to taste.

5. Pack the mixture into the onions, mounding any surplus over the tops, and place the onions in a shallow ovenproof dish. Pour the stock round the onions and cover the dish with lightly oiled cooking foil.

6. Bake at 350°F/180°C (Gas Mark 4) for about 45 minutes.

7. Trim the crusts from the bread, cut it into cubes and fry these in a little butter until crisp.

8. Lift the onions out with a draining spoon. Arrange them on a serving dish, scatter the bread cubes over them and serve with a tomato sauce.

STUFFED CABBAGE LEAVES I

Imperial (Metric)	American
1 medium onion	1 medium onion
1 clove garlic	1 clove garlic
Vegetable oil	Vegetable oil
4 oz (100g) mushrooms, chopped	1½ cupsful chopped mushrooms
1 oz (25g) walnuts, chopped	¼ cupful chopped English walnuts
½ oz (15g) pine nuts	1½ tablespoonsful pine nuts
2 tablespoonsful tomato *purée*	2 tablespoonsful tomato paste
1 teaspoonful chopped fresh marjoram or ½ teaspoonful dried marjoram	1 teaspoonful chopped fresh marjoram or ½ teaspoonful dried marjoram
1 teaspoonful chopped fresh lovage or ½ teaspoonsful dried lovage (optional)	1 teaspoonful chopped fresh lovage or ½ teaspoonful dried lovage (optional)
2 teaspoonsful chopped parsley	2 teaspoonsful chopped parsley
4 oz (100g) cooked brown rice	⅔ cupful cooked brown rice
Seasoning to taste	Seasoning to taste
8 cabbage leaves	8 cabbage leaves
1 oz (25g) sultanas	2 tablespoonsful golden seedless raisins
1 oz (25g) almonds, blanched and chopped	¼ cupful chopped blanched almonds
½ pint (¼ litre) vegetable stock (page 29)	1⅓ cupsful vegetable stock (page 29)
Spicy Tomato Sauce (page 28)	Spicy Tomato Sauce (page 28)

1. Peel the onion and garlic and chop finely. Fry them gently in a little oil for 5 minutes or until beginning to soften.

2. Add the mushrooms, walnuts and pine nuts to the onion mixture and cook for a further 5 minutes. Stir in the tomato *purée*, herbs and cooked rice and season to taste.

3. Blanch the cabbage leaves in boiling water for 2 minutes and drain well. Spread them out on a board and divide the stuffing between them.

4. Roll these up, tucking in edges, to make parcels. Pack them into

a shallow ovenproof dish and sprinkle with sultanas and chopped almonds.

5. Pour in the stock, cover and bake at 375°F/190°C (Gas Mark 5) for about 30 minutes.

6. Lift the parcels out carefully with a draining spoon and serve with Spicy Tomato sauce.

STUFFED CABBAGE LEAVES II

Imperial (Metric)	American
2 oz (50g) walnuts	½ cupful English walnuts
2 oz (50g) cooked chestnuts	½ cupful cooked chestnuts
4 oz (100g) cooked beans or chick peas	⅔ cupful cooked beans or garbanzo beans
4 oz (100g) cottage cheese	½ cupful cottage cheese
2 oz (50g) grated Cheddar cheese or Parmesan	½ cupful grated Cheddar cheese or Parmesan
1 clove garlic, peeled and crushed	1 clove garlic, peeled and crushed
1 tablespoonful chopped mint	1 tablespoonful chopped mint
Seasoning to taste	Seasoning to taste
Paprika to taste	Paprika to taste
8 cabbage leaves	8 cabbage leaves
½ pint (¼ litre) vegetable stock (page 29)	1⅓ cupsful vegetable stock (page 29)
2-3 oz (50-75g) dried apricots, washed, soaked and cut in small pieces	½ cupful dried apricots, washed, soaked and cut in small pieces
Fruity Sauce (page 25)	Fruity Sauce (page 25)

1. Mill or grind the walnuts and chestnuts. If chestnuts are not available use 4 ounces (100g) walnuts. Mash or mill the cooked beans or chick peas (garbanzo beans).

2. Mix the nuts and mashed beans with the cottage cheese, grated cheese, garlic, mint, salt and pepper and paprika.

3. Blanch the cabbage leaves and proceed as in the previous recipe, cooking the stuffed leaves with the stock and apricots.

4. Lift the stuffed leaves out with draining spoon, arrange the apricot pieces on top and serve with Fruity Sauce.

STUFFED PEPPER CASSEROLE I

Imperial (Metric)	American
4 medium green peppers	4 medium green peppers
1½ oz (40g) onion, finely chopped	¼ cupful onion, finely chopped
1 stick celery, finely chopped	1 stalk celery, finely chopped
½ lb (¼ kilo) tinned tomatoes	1 small can tomatoes
2 oz (50g) salted peanuts, chopped	½ cupful chopped salted peanuts
3 oz (75g) cooked long-grain brown rice	½ cupful cooked long-grain brown rice
Seasoning to taste	Seasoning to taste
2 tablespoonsful dry wholemeal breadcrumbs	2 tablespoonsful dry wholewheat breadcrumbs
¼ pint (150ml) vegetable stock (page 29)	⅔ cupful vegetable stock (page 29)

1. Remove the stem ends from the peppers and take out the seeds. Blanch the peppers for 5 minutes in boiling salted water and drain well.

2. Melt the margarine in a pan and fry the onion and celery gently for 5 minutes. Add the tomatoes and their juice, bring to the boil and simmer for 10 minutes.

3. Stir in the chopped peanuts and the cooked rice and season to taste with salt and pepper.

4. Stuff the peppers with the mixture and place them upright in a small baking tin or ovenproof dish. Top with the breadcrumbs and pour a little stock round the peppers.

5. Cover with a piece of lightly oiled cooking foil and bake at 350°F/180°C (Gas Mark 4) for about 30-40 minutes, removing the foil for the last 10 minutes of cooking.

STUFFED PEPPER CASSEROLE II

Imperial (Metric)	American
4 medium green peppers	4 medium green peppers
1 medium onion	1 medium onion
3 sticks celery	3 stalks celery
4 oz (100g) mushrooms	2 cupsful mushrooms
2 oz (50g) butter or polyunsaturated margarine	¼ cupful butter or polyunsaturated margarine
1 teaspoonful chopped parsley	1 teaspoonful chopped parsley
Good pinch dried sage	Good pinch dried sage
1 tablespoonful tomato *purée*	1 tablespoonful tomato paste
Pinch chilli powder	Pinch chili powder
½ pint (¼ litre) natural yogurt	1⅓ cupsful natural yogurt
4 tablespoonsful wholemeal breadcrumbs	4 tablespoonsful wholewheat breadcrumbs
Seasoning to taste	Seasoning to taste
¼ pint (150ml) vegetable stock (page 29)	⅔ cupful vegetable stock (page 29)
Tomato Sauce (page 27)	Tomato Sauce (page 27)

1. Cut the peppers in half lengthwise and remove the seeds. Blanch the peppers for 5 minutes in boiling salted water and drain well.

2. Peel and chop the onion. Chop the celery and mushrooms. Fry together in butter or margarine for about 5 minutes, stirring well.

3. Add the herbs, tomato *purée* and chilli powder and mix in the yogurt, reserving 4 tablespoonsful for the topping. Add enough breadcrumbs to give a firm, but not dry, mixture. Season with salt and pepper.

4. Fill the peppers with the stuffing and arrange them in an ovenproof dish. Pour a little stock round the peppers and cover.

5. Bake at 375°F/190°C (Gas Mark 5) for 30 minutes, then top each pepper with a spoonful of the remaining yogurt and bake uncovered for a further 10 minutes. Serve with tomato sauce.

STUFFED MARROW I

Imperial (Metric)	American
1 medium marrow	1 medium summer squash
1 large onion	1 large onion
1 stick celery	1 stalk celery
4 oz (100g) butter or polyunsaturated margarine	½ cupful butter or polyunsaturated margarine
3 oz (75g) wholemeal breadcrumbs	1½ cupsful wholewheat breadcrumbs
2 teaspoonsful grated lemon rind	2 teaspoonsful grated lemon rind
1 tablespoonful chopped parsley	1 tablespoonful chopped parsley
2-3 sage leaves, chopped	2-3 sage leaves, chopped
1 medium cooking apple	1 medium cooking apple
Seasoning to taste	Seasoning to taste
¼ pint (150ml) vegetable stock (page 29)	⅔ cupful vegetable stock (page 29)
2-3 tablespoonsful white wine	2-3 tablespoonsful white wine
2 tablespoonsful pine nuts	2 tablespoonsful pine nuts

1. Peel the marrow (squash) and cut off the ends. Divide it into sections about 2½-3 in. (6-8cm) thick. Scrape the seeds out carefully and blanch the sections in boiling salted water for 5 minutes so that the flesh begins to soften slightly. Drain well.

2. Peel and chop the onion, clean and chop the celery and fry them gently in half the butter or margarine until they begin to soften.

3. Add half the remaining butter and melt gently. Stir in the breadcrumbs, lemon rind, parsley and sage leaves. Peel, core and chop the cooking apple and add it to the mixture. Season well with salt and pepper.

4. Pack the filling into the marrow (squash) sections, place them in a casserole, dot with the remaining butter and pour in the stock and wine.

5. Cover the marrow (squash) loosely with foil and bake at 375°F/190°C (Gas Mark 5) for about 1 hour, basting occasionally with the stock and wine. About 15 minutes before the end of

cooking, uncover the dish and sprinkle the marrow (squash) with chopped pine nuts.

STUFFED MARROW II

Imperial (Metric)
1 medium marrow
6 dried prunes, soaked overnight,
   stoned and chopped
1 large apple
1 oz (25g) chopped walnuts
3 oz (75g) wholemeal breadcrumbs
Grated rind of ½ lemon
Lemon juice to taste
Seasoning to taste
1½ oz (40g) butter or
   polyunsaturated margarine
¼ pint (150ml) vegetable stock
   (page 29)
1 tablespoonful dry wholemeal
   breadcrumbs

American
1 medium summer squash
6 dried prunes, soaked overnight,
   stoned and chopped
1 large apple
¼ cupful chopped English walnuts
1½ cupsful wholewheat
   breadcrumbs
Grated rind of ½ lemon
Lemon juice to taste
Seasoning to taste
4 tablespoonsful butter or
   polyunsaturated margarine
⅔ cupful vegetable stock (page 29)
1 tablespoonful dry wholewheat
   breadcrumbs

1. Prepare and blanch the marrow (squash) as in preceding recipe.

2. Peel, core and chop the apple. Mix with the chopped prunes and walnuts and the breadcrumbs, lemon rind and juice, and seasoning to taste. Beat the egg and add just enough to bind the mixture.

3. Stuff the marrow (squash) sections with the breadcrumb mixture and dot with butter. Place them in a casserole, pour the stock round and continue as in preceding recipe.

4. Fry the dry breadcrumbs in remaining butter and scatter over the marrow (squash) sections before serving.

Note: This amount will serve 2 as a main course, 4 as a light meal or starter.

5.

PASTRY DISHES

MUSHROOM AND POTATO PIE

Imperial (Metric)	American
1½ lb (¾ kilo) potatoes	1½ pounds potatoes
Milk	Milk
Butter or polyunsaturated margarine	Butter or polyunsaturated margarine
Seasoning to taste	Seasoning to taste
½ lb (¼ kilo) mushrooms	4 cupsful mushrooms
1 tablespoonful chopped parsley	1 tablespoonful chopped parsley
½ teaspoonful dried tarragon	½ teaspoonful dried tarragon
Pinch dried basil	Pinch dried basil
Flaky pastry made with 6 oz (150g) wholemeal flour (page 15)	Flaky pastry made with 1½ cupsful wholewheat flour (page 15)

1. Scrub the potatoes, cut them into even sized pieces and cook them in boiling salted water. Drain well, skin, and mash them with a little hot milk and a generous knob of butter or margarine. Season with salt and pepper.

2. Slice the mushrooms thickly and fry them until soft in butter or margarine.

3. Spoon the mashed potatoes into a pie dish and top with the mushrooms. Sprinkle with the herbs. Leave it to cool.

4. Roll out the pastry, cover the pie, seal and crimp the edges.

5. Bake the pie at 425°F/220°C (Gas Mark 7) for 15 minutes, then reduce heat to 350°F/180°C (Gas Mark 4) for a further 10 minutes.

MUSHROOM ROLL-UP

Imperial (Metric)	American
1 small leek	1 small leek
1 medium onion	1 medium onion
1 clove garlic	1 clove garlic
2 oz (50g) butter	¼ cupful butter
1 tablespoonful vegetable oil	1 tablespoonful vegetable oil
6 oz (150g) mushrooms	3 cupsful mushrooms
4 tablespoonsful wholemeal breadcrumbs	4 tablespoonsful wholewheat breadcrumbs
1 teaspoonful dried tarragon	1 teaspoonful dried tarragon
Seasoning to taste	Seasoning to taste
2 tablespoonsful soured cream	2 tablespoonsful soured cream
Flaky or Quick 'Flaky' pastry made with 6 oz (150g) 81% wholemeal flour (pages 15 and 16)	Flaky or Quick 'Flaky' pastry made with 1½ cupsful 81% wholewheat flour (pages 15 and 16)

1. Trim, wash and chop the leek. Blanch it in boiling salted water for 3-4 minutes, or until it begins to soften. Drain, pressing out all the cooking liquid.

2. Peel and chop the onion and garlic and fry them gently in the butter and oil until beginning to soften. Chop the mushrooms, add them to the onion and cook until the mushrooms soften. If juices run from the mushrooms, turn the heat up to dry the mixture out, stirring well. Transfer the mushrooms to a basin with the leeks to cool, then chop the vegetables finely.

3. Add the breadcrumbs and tarragon and season well with salt and pepper. Stir in the soured cream.

4. Roll the pastry out thinly to form a rectangle. Spread it with the filling, leaving a 1 in. (2.5cm) space round the edges. Roll it up and seal the edges.

5. Bake the roll at 425°F/220°C (Gas Mark 7) for 15 minutes, then reduce the heat to 350°F/180°C (Gas Mark 4) for 15-20 minutes.

SUMMERTIME CREAM CHEESE PIE

Imperial (Metric)	American
Shortcrust pastry made with ½ lb (¼ kilo) 81% wholemeal flour (page 13)	Shortcrust pastry made with 2 cupsful 81% wholewheat flour (page 13)
6 oz (150g) cream cheese	⅔ cupful cream cheese
2 oz (50g) Cheddar cheese, grated	½ cupful grated cheese
Good pinch grated nutmeg	Good pinch grated nutmeg
Dash Tabasco sauce	Dash Tabasco sauce
Seasoning to taste	Seasoning to taste
1 tablespoonful single cream or top of milk	1 tablespoonful single cream or top of milk
4 eggs	4 eggs
2 tablespoonsful finely chopped mint	2 tablespoonsful finely chopped mint
2-3 tomatoes	2-3 tomatoes

1. Beat the cream cheese with a fork and gradually work in the grated cheese, seasonings and cream.

2. Roll out the pastry and use half to line an 8 in. (20cm) pie plate.

3. Spread the cheese mixture over the pastry. Make 4 hollows in the mixture and carefully break an egg into each. Sprinkle with chopped mint and season with salt and pepper.

4. Cover the pie with the remaining pastry, seal the edges and bake at 425°F/220°C (Gas Mark 7) for 15 minutes. Lower the heat to 350°F/180°C (Gas Mark 4) for a further 15 minutes.

5. Remove the pie from the oven. Slice the tomatoes thinly. When the pie has cooled and is just warm, garnish with a ring of tomato slices before serving. It may also be eaten cold.

SAVOURY PUMPKIN PIE

Imperial (Metric)	American
1½-2 lb (¾-1 kilo) pumpkin	1½-2 pounds pumpkin
1 medium onion	1 medium onion
2 cloves garlic	2 cloves garlic
2 oz (50g) butter	5 tablespoonsful butter
Dash of Tabasco sauce	Dash of Tabasco sauce
1 tablespoonful soy sauce	1 tablespoonful soy sauce
1 teaspoonful ground ginger	1 teaspoonful ground ginger
¼ teaspoonful each ground cinnamon and nutmeg	¼ teaspoonful each ground cinnamon and nutmeg
Seasoning to taste	Seasoning to taste
½ lb (¼ kilo) cooked dried white beans or chick peas	1 cupful cooked dried white beans or garbanzo beans
6 oz (150g) grated cheese	1½ cupsful grated cheese
2 oz (50g) chopped walnuts	½ cupful chopped English walnuts
Shortcrust pastry made with 6 oz (150g) 81% wholemeal flour (page 13)	Shortcrust pastry made with 1½ cupsful 81% wholewheat flour (page 13)

1. Peel and cube the pumpkin and cook it in boiling salted water until tender. Drain well and mash it.

2. Peel the onion and garlic and chop finely. Fry them in butter over a medium heat until transparent. Mix them with the pumpkin *purée* and season with Tabasco, spices, soy sauce and salt and pepper.

3. Mash the beans and add them to the mixture. Beat in the grated cheese. (The beans may be sieved to remove the skins if you wish.)

4. Transfer the mixture to a pie dish. Roll out the pastry and cover the pie.

5. Bake the pie at 400°F/200°C (Gas Mark 6) for 15 minutes. Reduce the heat to 350°F/180°C (Gas Mark 4) for a further 15 minutes.

CHEESE AND OLIVE PIE

Imperial (Metric)	American
Quick 'Flaky' pastry made with ½ lb (¼ kilo) wholemeal flour (page 16)	Quick 'Flaky' pastry made with 2 cupsful wholewheat flour (page 16)
1 oz (25g) butter or polyunsaturated margarine	2½ tablespoonsful butter or polyunsaturated margarine
½ lb (¼ kilo) onions, thinly sliced	8 ounces onions, thinly sliced
12 stuffed green olives, sliced	12 stuffed green olives, sliced
2 large eggs	2 large eggs
½ pint (¼ litre) single cream	1⅓ cupsful light cream
Seasoning to taste	Seasoning to taste
4 oz (100g) Dutch cheese, grated	1 cupful Dutch cheese, grated

1. Roll out the pastry and line a 9 in. (23cm) pie plate or fluted flan tin. Re-roll the trimmings and cut into circles or crescents with a 2 in. (5cm) cutter. Chill the pastry lightly while preparing the filling.

2. Melt the butter or margarine in a small pan and cook the onions, covered, over gentle heat until soft but not brown. Remove the onions with a slotted spoon, draining well. Place them in the pastry case with the sliced olives.

3. Beat the eggs and mix them with the cream and seasoning. Pour this mixture over the onions and olives and sprinkle with the cheese. Arrange pastry circles on top.

4. Bake at 400°F/200°C (Gas Mark 6) for 15 minutes, then reduce the heat to 350°F/180°C (Gas Mark 4) for a further 25 minutes, or until the filling is set and golden brown.

BROAD BEAN AND CARROT PIE

Imperial (Metric)	American
4 oz (100g) broad beans, fresh, frozen or tinned	1 cupful Windsor beans, fresh, frozen or canned
1 large carrot, scraped and diced	1 large carrot, scraped and diced
Vegetable stock (page 29)	Vegetable stock (page 29)
Milk	Milk
1 oz (25g) butter or polyunsaturated margarine	2½ tablespoonsful butter or polyunsaturated margarine
1 oz (25g) plain 81% wholemeal flour	¼ cupful plain 81% wholewheat flour
1 tablespoonful chutney	1 tablespoonful chutney
1 medium onion, peeled and chopped	1 medium onion, peeled and chopped
Seasoning to taste	Seasoning to taste
Pinch of dry mustard powder	Pinch of dry mustard powder
6 oz (150g) Cheddar cheese, diced	1½ cupsful diced cheese
1 tablespoonful chopped parsley	1 tablespoonful chopped parsley
Quick 'Flaky' pastry made with ½ lb (¼ kilo) 81% wholemeal flour (page 16)	Quick 'Flaky' pastry made with 2 cupsful 81% wholewheat flour (page 16)

1. Cook the broad beans and carrot in just enough stock to cover. Drain, reserving the stock.

2. Make up a mixture of stock and milk to give ¼ pint (150ml), using approximately half stock, half milk. Make into a thick white sauce with the butter and flour (for method see page 23).

3. Remove the pan from the heat and stir in the chutney, chopped onion, cubed cheese and the cooked beans and carrots. Season with salt, pepper and mustard powder and stir in the chopped parsley. Cool.

4. Roll out half the pastry and line a 9 in. (23cm) pie plate. Spoon in the vegetable mixture, cover with the remaining pastry and seal well.

5. Bake at 425°F/220°C (Gas Mark 7) for 15 minutes, then reduce the heat to 350°F/180°C (Gas Mark 4) for a further 10-15 minutes.

LITTLE CURRIED PASTIES

Imperial (Metric)

Wholemeal pastry or Quick 'Flaky'
pastry made with ½ lb (225g)
wholemeal flour (see pages 14
and 16)
6 oz (150g) finely diced potato
2 oz (50g) chopped onion
Vegetable oil
2 teaspoonsful curry powder, or to
taste
1 medium apple
2 tablespoonsful sultanas
2 tablespoonsful cooked peas
Seasoning to taste
2 teaspoonsful chopped coriander or
parsley

American

Wholewheat pastry or Quick 'Flaky'
pastry made with 2 cupsful
wholewheat flour (see pages 14
and 16)
1 cupful finely diced potato
½ cupful chopped onion
Vegetable oil
2 teaspoonsful curry powder, or to
taste
1 medium apple
2 tablespoonsful golden seedless
raisins
2 tablespoonsful cooked peas
Seasoning to taste
2 teaspoonsful chopped cilantro or
parsley

1. Make the pastry using a little more water than usual to make a
   firm, non-crumbly dough.

2. Fry the potato and onion gently in the oil until beginning to soften.
   Sprinkle with the curry powder and fry for a further 4-5 minutes,
   stirring with a wooden spoon.

3. Peel and chop the apple and add it to the pan with the sultanas
   (golden seedless raisins). Stir all together for 3-4 minutes, then
   add a good pinch of salt and enough water to come halfway up
   the vegetables.

4. Cook gently, uncovered, until the mixture is soft and the liquid
   has been absorbed, adding the peas for the last few minutes of
   cooking. Allow to cool completely. Add herbs and seasoning to
   taste.

5. Roll the pastry out thinly and cut it into circles about 3½ in. (9cm)
   across. A large cup is a useful size cutter.

6. Divide the filling between half the pastry circles, cover with the remaining circles and seal the edges well.

7. Heat the oil for deep frying and fry the pasties a few at a time until they are brown and crisp. Drain them well on kitchen paper.

Note: The pasties may be baked in the oven if you wish, but frying gives a particularly good flavour and texture.

CHEESE AND CHUTNEY PASTIES

Imperial (Metric)	American
½ lb (250g) cottage cheese	1 cupful cottage cheese
1 large egg, beaten	1 large egg, beaten
2 oz (50g) 81% wholemeal flour	½ cupful 81% wholewheat flour
2 oz (50g) grated onion	Grated onion
4 oz (100g) chopped walnuts	1 cupful chopped English walnuts
1 tablespoonful chutney or sweet pickle	1 tablespoonful chutney or sweet pickle
Sea salt to taste	Sea salt to taste
Dash of Tabasco sauce	Dash of Tabasco sauce
Quick 'Flaky' pastry made with ½ lb (50g) wholemeal flour (see page 16)	Quick 'Flaky' pastry made with 2 cupsful wholewheat flour (see page 16)

1. Beat up the cottage cheese well with a fork and mix in the beaten egg and the flour.

2. Stir in the grated onion, chopped walnuts and chutney. Season to taste with salt and Tabasco.

3. Roll the pastry out thinly and cut into 8 circles. Divide filling into 8. Place on the pastry and fold over and seal as for 'turnovers'.

4. Bake at 425°F/220°C (Gas Mark 7) for 10 minutes, then lower heat to 350°F/180°C (Gas Mark 4) for a further 10-15 minutes.

TOMATO AND MUSHROOM PIE

Imperial (Metric)	American
Shortcrust pastry made with ½ lb (¼ kilo) 81% wholemeal flour (page 13)	Shortcrust pastry made with 2 cupsful 81% wholewheat flour (page 13)
1 lb (½ kilo) firm tomatoes	1 pound firm tomatoes
1 medium onion	1 medium onion
4 oz (100g) mushrooms	2 cupsful mushrooms
4 oz (100g) grated cheese	1 cupful grated cheese
1 teaspoonful dried marjoram	1 teaspoonful dried marjoram
1 teaspoonful dry mustard	1 teaspoonful dry mustard
Seasoning to taste	Seasoning to taste

1. Roll out the pastry and use half to line the base of a 9 in. (23cm) pie plate.

2. Slice the tomatoes thinly, cut the onion into thin rings and chop the mushrooms roughly.

3. Mix together the grated cheese, marjoram, mustard, salt and pepper. Place a layer of tomatoes and mushrooms on the pastry, cover with onion rings and sprinkle with the mixed cheese and herbs. Repeat the layers with the remaining ingredients.

4. Cover the pie with the remaining pastry. Seal the edges, crimp decoratively and cut a cross in the centre of the pie.

5. Bake at 400°F/200°C (Gas Mark 6) for 15 minutes, then turn the heat down to 350°F/180°C (Gas Mark 4) for 15 minutes.

ARTICHOKE PIE

Imperial (Metric)	American
1 lb (½ kilo) Jerusalem artichokes	1 pound Jerusalem artichokes
1 lb (½ kilo) potatoes	1 pound potatoes
Milk	Milk
½ oz (50g) butter	1½ tablespoonsful butter
Seasoning to taste	Seasoning to taste
Cheese Sauce made with ½ pint (¼ litre) milk and vegetable water (page 24)	Cheese Sauce made with 1⅓ cupsful milk and vegetable water (page 24)
1 tablespoonful chopped parsley	1 tablespoonful chopped parsley
2 eggs, hard-boiled	2 eggs, hard-boiled
2 oz (50g) chopped walnuts	½ cupful chopped English walnuts
Flaky pastry made with ½ lb (¼ kilo) 81% wholemeal flour (page 15)	Flaky pastry made with 2 cupsful 81% wholewheat flour (page 15)

1. Peel the artichokes and cook them in lightly salted boiling water until tender. Drain, reserving the cooking liquid. Mash the artichokes and reserve.

2. Scrub the potatoes, cut them into even sized pieces and cook them in boiling salted water until tender. Drain and mash them with a little hot milk and the butter. Season with salt and pepper.

3. Make the cheese sauce, using half milk and half cooking water from the artichokes. Mix with the chopped parsley and fold in the chopped hard-boiled eggs.

4. Make layers of mashed potato, artichokes and hard-boiled egg mixture in a greased pie dish, sprinkling with chopped walnuts and seasoning lightly.

5. Cover with the pastry. Bake at 425°F(220°C (Gas Mark 7) for 15 minutes, then reduce the heat to 325°F/170°C (Gas Mark 3) for a further 20 minutes.

CHEESY LEEK PIE

Imperial (Metric)	American
2 medium leeks	2 medium leeks
1 medium onion	1 medium onion
1 clove garlic	1 clove garlic
Vegetable oil	Vegetable oil
Shortcrust pastry made with ½ lb (¼ kilo) 81% wholemeal flour (page 13)	Shortcrust pastry made with 2 cupsful 81% wholewheat flour (page 13)
6 oz (150g) cooked long grain brown rice	1 cupful cooked long grain brown rice
2 eggs, hard-boiled and chopped	2 eggs, hard-boiled and chopped
2-3 oz (50-75g) Cheddar cheese, diced	1 cupful Cheddar cheese, diced
1 bunch watercress, well washed and chopped	1 bunch watercress, well washed and chopped
2 teaspoonsful chopped parsley	2 teaspoonsful chopped parsley
1 teaspoonful chopped basil (optional)	1 teaspoonful chopped basil (optional)
Seasoning to taste	Seasoning to taste

1. Trim the leeks and wash well. Cut them into short lengths and cook them in boiling salted water until just tender. Drain them, pressing out as much water as possible.

2. Peel and chop the onion and garlic and fry them gently in a little oil until they begin to soften.

3. Roll out the pastry and use half to line a deep pie plate. Spread the cooked rice over the base of the pie.

4. Mix together the leek and onions, the chopped hard boiled eggs, diced cheese, chopped watercress, herbs and seasoning.

5. Spread the mixture over the rice. Roll out the remaining pastry, cover the pie and seal.

6. Bake the pie at 400°F/200°C (Gas Mark 6) for 15 minutes, then reduce the heat to 350°F/180°C (Gas Mark 4) for a further 15 minutes.

RED CABBAGE AND MUSHROOM PIE

Imperial (Metric)	American
2 eggs	2 eggs
Shortcrust pastry made with ½ lb (¼ kilo) 81% wholemeal flour (page 13)	Shortcrust pastry made with 2 cupsful 81% wholewheat flour (page 13)
½ lb (¼ kilo) mushrooms	4 cupsful mushrooms
3 oz (75g) butter	7½ tablespoonsful butter
2 medium onions	2 medium onions
1 lb (½ kilo) red cabbage	1 pound red cabbage
½ teaspoonful dried marjoram or thyme	½ teaspoonful dried marjoram or thyme
Seasoning to taste	Seasoning to taste
3 oz (75g) cream cheese	¾ cupful cream cheese
Tangy Apple Sauce (page 26)	Tangy Apple Sauce (page 26)

1. Hard-boil the eggs, crack their shells and cool them under running cold water. Roll out pastry and use half to line a deep 9 in. (23cm) pie plate.

2. Slice the mushrooms if large. Fry them briskly in half the butter until they begin to soften. Transfer to a bowl.

3. Peel and slice the onions, slice the cabbage thinly. Fry them together in the remaining butter with the herbs, stirring well, until soft. Season to taste with salt and pepper.

4. Spread the cream cheese on the base of the pie dish. Peel and slice the eggs and make a layer on top of the cheese. Season lightly. Cover with the cabbage mixture. Spoon the mushrooms over the top.

5. Cover with the remaining pastry. Seal the edges, crimp decoratively and bake at 400°F/200°C (Gas Mark 6) for 20 minutes. Reduce the heat to 350°F/180°C (Gas Mark 4) for a further 15-20 minutes. Serve with apple sauce.

PARSLEY AND EGG PIE

Imperial (Metric)	American
Quick 'Flaky' pastry made with ½ lb (¼ kilo) 81% wholemeal flour (page 16)	Quick 'Flaky' pastry made with 2 cupsful 81% wholewheat flour (page 16)
2 oz (50g) parsley, coarsely chopped	2 cupsful chopped parsley
4 tablespoonsful double cream	4 tablespoonsful heavy cream
4 eggs	4 eggs
Seasoning to taste	Seasoning to taste

1. Make the pastry and chill lightly.

2. Mix half the chopped parsley with the cream and season lightly.

3. Roll out half the pastry and line an 8 in. (20cm) pie plate. Spoon in the parsley and cream mixture.

3. Make shallow depressions in the parsley and break the eggs in carefully. Season well and scatter with the remaining parsley.

4. Cover with the rest of the pastry, trim, seal and crimp the edges.

5. Bake at 400°F/200°C (Gas Mark 6) for 20 minutes.

APPLE AND CELERY PIE

Imperial (Metric)	American
4 oz (100g) celery	4 ounces celery
White sauce made with ½ pint (250ml) mixed milk and cooking water from celery (for method see page 23)	White sauce made with 1⅓ cupsful mixed milk and cooking water from celery (for method see page 23
1 lb (500g) potatoes, cooked and mashed	1 pound potatoes, cooked and mashed
4 oz (100g) walnuts, chopped	1 cupful chopped walnuts
4 oz (100g) apple, peeled and chopped	4 ounces apple, peeled and chopped
2 oz (50g) cheese, cut into small cubes	2 ounces cheese, cut into small cubes
Shortcrust or wholemeal pastry made with 6 oz (150g) wholemeal flour (see pages 13 and 14)	Shortcrust or wholewheat pastry made with 1½ cupsful wholwheat flour (see pages 13 and 14)

1. Wash and trim celery and chop roughly. Cook in salted water to cover until just tender. Drain well and reserve cooking water.

2. Make the white sauce, using half milk and half the reserved liquid from the celery.

3. Mix the nuts, apple and cheese cubes with the white sauce and stir in the cooked celery.

4. Spread the mashed potatoes over the base of a deep pie plate. Cover with the white sauce mixture.

5. Roll out the pastry, cover the pie and bake at 400°F/200°C (Gas Mark 6) for 15 minutes, then lower heat to 350°F/180°C (Gas Mark 4) for a further 15 minutes.

ONION AND APPLE PIE

Imperial (Metric)	American
1 lb (½ kilo) cooking apples	1 pound cooking apples
2 medium onions	2 medium onions
Shortcrust pastry made with 4 oz (100g) 81% wholemeal flour (page 13)	Shortcrust pastry made with 1 cupful 81% wholewheat flour (page 13)
4 oz (100g) cheese, grated	1 cupful grated cheese
2 eggs	2 eggs
½ pint (¼ litre) milk or a mixture of milk and cream	1⅓ cupsful milk or a mixture of milk and cream
Seasoning to taste	Seasoning to taste
2-3 tomatoes	2-3 tomatoes
Cheesy Crumb Topping (page 17)	Cheesy Crumb Topping (page 17)

1. Peel, core and slice the apples. Peel and chop the onions. Cook them together in a little water until tender. Drain well and cool.

2. Roll out the pastry and line a 9 in. (23cm) pie plate. Spoon in the apple and onion mixture. Sprinkle with the cheese.

3. Beat the eggs and mix with the milk. Season and pour over the filling.

4. Bake at 425°F/220°C (Gas Mark 7) for 10 minutes, then lower the heat to 350°F/170°C (Gas Mark 3) and bake for a further 15 minutes.

5. Remove the pie carefully from the oven, slice the tomatoes and arrange them over the filling. Sprinkle with the Cheesy Crumb Topping.

6. Replace the pie in the oven for a further 15 minutes or until the filling is set.

RATATOUILLE PIE

Imperial (Metric)	American
¾ lb (350g) courgettes	12 ounces zucchini
4 oz (100g) aubergine	4 ounces eggplant
1 medium onion	1 medium onion
1 clove garlic	1 clove garlic
Vegetable oil	Vegetable oil
4 oz (100g) tomatoes	4 ounces tomatoes
2 teaspoonsful chopped parsley	2 teaspoonsful chopped parsley
½ teaspoonful each chopped rosemary and marjoram	½ teaspoonful each chopped rosemary and marjoram
Seasoning to taste	Seasoning to taste
Quick 'Flaky' pastry made with 6 oz (150g) 81% wholemeal flour (page 16)	Quick 'Flaky' pastry made with 1½ cupsful 81% wholewheat flour (page 16)
2 oz (50g) grated cheese	½ cupful grated cheese
4 stuffed olives	4 stuffed olives

1. Trim and chop the courgettes (zucchini) and aubergine (eggplant). Peel and chop the onion. Peel and crush the garlic. Heat a little oil in a pan and stir-fry the chopped vegetables over a medium heat for a few minutes. Skin and chop the tomatoes and add them to the pan.

2. Add the herbs, cover and cook over very low heat, stirring occasionally, until all the vegetables are soft (about 30 minutes). Season to taste with salt and pepper. Cool.

3. While the vegetables are cooking, roll out the pastry and line a 9 in. (23cm) pie plate. Re-roll the trimmings and cut into circles or crescents with a 2 in. (5cm) cutter.

4. Spoon the ratatouille into the pastry case and top with the grated cheese and the olives cut into pieces.

5. Arrange pastry circles on top of the cheese and olives and bake the pie at 400°F/200°C (Gas Mark 6) for about 20 minutes or until it is hot through and lightly browned.

SYRIAN SPINACH PIE

Imperial (Metric)

Wholemeal pastry made with 6 oz (150g) flour (page 14)
1 lb (½ kilo) spinach
Cheese Sauce made with ¼ pint (150ml) milk (page 24)
¼ teaspoonful grated nutmeg
½ oz (15g) polyunsaturated margarine
2 oz (50g) sultanas
1 oz (25g) pine nuts
Seasoning to taste
Cheesy Crumb Topping (page 17)
2 tablespoonsful sesame seeds, toasted

American

Wholewheat pastry made with 1½ cupsful flour (page 14)
1 pound spinach
Cheese Sauce made with 1⅓ cupsful milk (page 24)
¼ teaspoonful grated nutmeg
1½ tablespoonsful polyunsaturated margarine
⅓ cupful golden seedless raisins
¼ cupful pine nuts
Seasoning to taste
Cheesy Crumb Topping (page 17)
2 tablespoonsful sesame seeds, toasted

1. Roll out the pastry and line a 9 in. (23cm) pie plate. Prick the base well with a fork and bake 'blind' at 400°F/200°C (Gas Mark 6) for about 15 minutes.

2. Meanwhile, wash the spinach thoroughly and cook it in a covered pan using just the water clinging to the leaves. Drain, pressing out as much liquid as possible, and chop the spinach.

3. Make the cheese sauce, stir in the spinach and nutmeg.

4. Heat the margarine in a small pan and fry the sultanas and pine nuts briskly for a few minutes.

5. Add the sultanas and pine nuts to the spinach mixture and season to taste. Spoon the mixture into the pastry case and sprinkle with the Cheesy Crumb Topping.

6. Bake at 375°F/190°C (Gas Mark 5) for 15 minutes. Sprinkle the toasted sesame seeds on top before serving.

SPINACH PIE WITH APPLE AND HERBS

Imperial (Metric)	American
1 lb (½ kilo) fresh spinach or equivalent in frozen spinach	1 pound fresh spinach or equivalent in frozen spinach
¾ lb (300g) cooking apples	12 ounces cooking apples
Seasoning to taste	Seasoning to taste
Pinch grated nutmeg	Pinch grated nutmeg
Pinch dried marjoram	Pinch dried marjoram
Pinch dried basil	Pinch dried basil
1 medium onion, chopped	1 medium onion, chopped
Vegetable oil	Vegetable oil
Shortcrust pastry made with 6 oz (150g) 81% wholemeal flour (page 13)	Shortcrust pastry made with 1½ cupsful 81% wholewheat flour (page 13)
1 small egg, beaten	1 small egg, beaten
3 tomatoes, sliced	3 tomatoes, sliced
6-8 stuffed olives, sliced	6-8 stuffed olives, sliced
Chopped parsley	Chopped parsley

1. Wash the spinach well, shake it, and cook it in the moisture clinging to the leaves. Cook frozen spinach according to the package directions. Drain it well, press out any remaining water and chop it roughly.

2. Peel, core and chop the apples and cook them with 1-2 tablespoonsful water until soft. Mash them and mix with the spinach. Cool and season with salt, pepper and herbs.

3. Fry the chopped onion gently in a little oil until soft. Mix it with the spinach and apple.

4. Roll out the pastry and line a 9 in. (23cm) pie plate. Re-roll the trimmings and cut into circles or crescents using a 2 in. (5cm) cutter.

5. Brush the inside of pastry case with beaten egg, prick the base well with a fork and bake at 400°F/200°C (Gas Mark 6) for 5 minutes and remove from the oven.

6. Spread the base with the spinach, apple and onion mixture. Top with the sliced tomatoes, olives and a sprinkling of parsley. Arrange the pastry circles on top.

7. Bake at 400°F/200°C (Gas Mark 6) for 15 minutes. Reduce the heat to 325°F/170°C (Gas Mark 3) for a further 15 minutes.

BROCCOLI NUT PIE

Imperial (Metric)	American
½ lb (¼ kilo) broccoli	8 ounces broccoli
2 oz (50g) blanched almonds, chopped	½ cupful chopped blanched almonds
1 oz (25g) butter	2½ tablespoonsful butter
1 oz (25g) plain wholemeal flour	¼ cupful plain wholewheat flour
¼ pint (150ml) milk	⅔ cupful milk
Seasoning	Seasoning
3 oz (75g) Cheddar cheese, grated	¾ cupful grated cheese
Shortcrust pastry made with 4 oz (150g) wholemeal flour (page 13)	Shortcrust pastry made with 1 cupful wholewheat flour (page 13)

1. Trim the broccoli and cook it in boiling salted water until just tender. Drain it well, reserving the cooking liquid.

2. Toast the chopped almonds under a moderate grill until golden.

3. Make a thick white sauce with the butter, flour and the milk mixed with 2-3 tablespoonsful cooking liquid from the broccoli (for method see page 23). Season with salt and pepper. Stir in the grated cheese and toasted almonds.

4. Place the broccoli in a pie dish and pour the sauce over.

5. Roll out the pastry and cut into circles or crescents. Arrange them on top of the pie.

6. Bake at 400°F/200°C (Gas Mark 6) for 15 minutes. Reduce the heat to 325°F/170°C (Gas Mark 3) for a further 15 minutes.

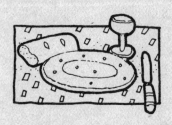

WALNUT AND PARSNIP PIE

Imperial (Metric)
Wholemeal pastry made with 4 oz
    (100g) flour (page 14)
4 oz (100g) chopped parsnip
1 medium onion, finely chopped
1 oz (25g) polyunsaturated
    margarine
1 oz (25g) wholemeal flour
¼ pint (150ml) thin cream or top of
    milk
1 oz (25g) wholemeal breadcrumbs
2 oz (50g) walnuts, chopped
Seasoning to taste
Good pinch ground nutmeg
Pinch curry powder
Chopped parsley

American
Wholewheat pastry made with
    1 cupful flour (page 14)
¾ cupful chopped parsnip
1 medium onion, finely chopped
2½ tablespoonsful polyunsaturatd
    margarine
¼ cupful wholewheat flour
⅔ cupful light cream or top of milk
½ cupful wholewheat breadcrumbs
½ cupful chopped English walnuts
Seasoning to taste
Good pinch ground nutmeg
Pinch curry powder
Chopped parsley

1. Make the pastry and chill it while preparing the filling.

2. Cook the parsnip in a little boiling water until it is soft. Drain
   well and mash.

3. Fry the onion gently in half the margarine until it begins to soften.
   Add the remaining margarine, remove from the heat and stir in
   the flour. Cook gently, stirring, for 2-3 minutes. Remove the pan
   from the heat, add the milk gradually and stir until it is smooth.
   Cook, stirring well, until it becomes thick. Leave it to cool.

4. Stir in the breadcrumbs, parsnip *purée*, nuts and seasonings.

5. Spoon the parsnip mixture into a 9 in. (23cm) pie plate. Roll out
   the pastry and cut it into circles or crescents, using a 2 in. (5cm)
   cutter. Arrange the pastry circles on top of the pie.

6. Bake the pie at 425°F/220°C (Gas Mark 7) for 15 minutes, then
   reduce the heat to 350°F/180°C (Gas Mark 4) for a further 15
   minutes. Sprinkle chopped parsley between the pastry circles
   before serving.

COTTAGE CHEESE SCONE WITH ONIONS

Imperial (Metric)	American
1 oz (25g) butter or polyunsaturated margarine	2½ tablespoonsful butter or polyunsaturated margarine
1 medium onion, sliced	1 medium onion, sliced
3 tomatoes, skinned and sliced	3 tomatoes, skinned and sliced
Seasoning to taste	Seasoning to taste
8 oz (225g) self-raising 81% wholemeal flour	2 cupsful self-raising 81% wholewheat flour
Pinch of sea salt	Pinch of sea salt
2 oz (50g) polyunsaturated margarine	¼ cupful polyunsaturated margarine
4 oz (100g) cottage cheese	½ cupful cottage cheese
1 egg	1 egg
2 tablespoonsful milk	2 tablespoonsful milk
4 black olives, stoned	4 black olives, stoned

1. Melt the butter or margarine in a pan and fry the onion gently for 5 minutes.

2. Grease an 8 in. (20cm) sandwich tin and line base with a circle of greaseproof paper. Arrange onions on top and cover with tomato slices. Season.

3. Make a scone dough by sifting the flour and salt together, returning to the bowl any bran left in the sieve, then rubbing in the margarine. Stir in the cottage cheese. Beat the egg with the milk, add to the rubbed-in mixture and mix to a soft dough.

4. Knead the dough lightly on a floured board and roll it out to an 8 in. (20cm) circle. Place it in the sandwich tin and press it down lightly over the tomatoes and onions.

5. Bake at 425°F/220°C (Gas Mark 7) for about 20 minutes, or until the scone dough is risen and brown. Turn it out of the tin, inverting it carefully onto a serving dish.

6. Remove the greaseproof paper and serve garnished with black olives.

INDEX